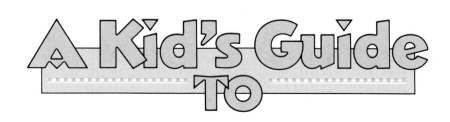

A Kid's Guide TO

Florida

GULLIVER
TRAVELS

A Kid's Guide
To

Florida

Gulliver Books

Harcourt Brace Jovanovich, Publishers

San Diego   New York   London

HBJ

ISBN 0-15-200461-0

Written by Karen Grove
Illustrations and maps by Richard E. Brown
Designed by G. B. D. Smith

Printed in the United States of America
First edition
A B C D E

C · O · N · T · E · N · T · S

How to Use This Book

If you're about to visit Florida, this is the book for you. Read it before you leave, then carry it with you while you're there so you can help choose where you want to go each day.

But don't just read it! Write in this book. Color some of the pictures. Keep track of your vacation in the travel diary. Use the maps: Try to figure out where you are and where you want to go. And there are games and puzzles all through the book for you to do while riding in a car or plane, waiting to eat, or just hanging around waiting for the grown-ups to get going!

T·R·A·V·E·L D·I·A·R·Y

My name is _____.

I live at _____.

in _____.

My phone number is (_____) _____ – _____

I'm taking a trip through Florida from _____

to _____. I'm traveling with _____

_____, and we plan to be away from home for _____ days.

My parents' full names are _____ and

_____. In case of an emergency,

they can be reached at _____,

or you can call _____ at

(_____) _____ – _____.

my picture

Birthday _____

Age _____

Sex _____

Height _____

Weight _____

Eye color _____

Hair color _____

The first part of the book tells you what it's like in Florida—about the warm, sunny weather, what to pack, the different ways you can get there, and how to get around once you've arrived.

Following this introduction is a fascinating chapter about the history of Florida. Did you know that there were European settlements here long before the Pilgrims ever landed at Plymouth Rock? Then there's a chapter about the wonderful variety of foods you can try on your trip, as well as a chapter on souvenir hunting.

Because Florida is such a large state, the next 7 sections each take a special look at the fun you can have in different areas of Florida—the Northeast Coast, Central Florida, the Southeast Coast, the

Florida Keys, the Everglades, the West Coast, and the Northwest/Panhandle region. Florida is a huge state, and there's more to do than you could ever imagine!

Once you know what month you'll be in the Sunshine State, take a look at the calendar on page 133 to discover what special annual events will be going on while you're there.

For particular information about a place you want to visit, like the address, the phone number, or the time it opens, look in the appendix. Following the appendix, you'll find a number of games you can play in the car, the answers to the puzzles in this book, and the index, where you can look up the page numbers for places and things you want to read about.

Use this book not only as a travel guide, but as a record of your trip. Color and draw wherever there's room. Write about the places you've visited. And remember, there are no right answers to put in the travel diary blanks. You can make up whatever you want!

In addition to filling in the travel diary, you may want to use a notebook to write down details of interesting or funny things that happen on your trip. Also, save your ticket stubs and brochures to tape into your journal. Leave room for photographs and your own illustrations. It's your journal, so be creative. It's a great way to remember your trip when it's over.

Did you know?

We've done our best to give you the latest information, but Florida is always changing and some of this information could change next week. You should always phone first to make sure the place you want to go is open.

AUG 8.
Today we went to Sea World! Mikey got sick at the dolphin show.
The whales were great and we saw a big Hammerhead SHARK!

Where Are We Going?

Northwest / Panhandle

Northeast Coast

Central Florida

West Coast

Southeast Coast

Everglades

Florida Keys

WELCOME TO PARADISE

Florida is a tropical paradise that welcomes the visitor. Whether you want a relaxing vacation of sun and water or an exciting whirlwind of man-made activities, Florida has what you're looking for. In fact, there's so much to do that you won't know where to start. Forget the idea of seeing it all . . . it's impossible. You'll have to pick out a few major things and save the rest for your next trip. Once you've had a taste of Florida, you're sure to return again and again.

Florida is the southernmost state in the continental United States. It's bordered by Alabama and Georgia to the north, the Atlantic Ocean to the east, the Caribbean Sea far to the south, and to the west, the Gulf of Mexico. Thirty thousand lakes and 166 rivers are contained in the 58,577 square miles of Florida. That's a lot of water!

Did you know?

When you cross the border into Florida, you are already 120 miles south of any beach in California.

5

Florida is called the "Sunshine State," and rightly so. Its climate draws hundreds of thousands of visitors each year to the tropical peninsula—some to vacation, others to set up home.

In winter, when many states are blanketed with snow and ice, people come to Florida to bask in the sun. But sun worshippers aren't the only ones who descend on the Sunshine State. Every spring, baseball comes to Florida, too.

Many of the major league teams hold their training camps in Florida. Here the players work out their winter kinks and practice for the season's opening in April.

The press and eager baseball fans attend exhibition games here in March and early April. If you're in Florida during spring training, check the newspaper for exhibition games. Most large cities play host to at least one major league team. This could be your opportunity to get those autographs missing from your collection!

Major League Baseball Spring Training

City	Team
Boardwalk and Baseball	Kansas City Royals
Bradenton	Pittsburgh Pirates
Clearwater	Philadelphia Phillies
Dunedin	Toronto Blue Jays
Fort Lauderdale	New York Yankees
Kissimmee	Houston Astros
Lakeland	Detroit Tigers
Miami	Baltimore Orioles
Orlando	Minnesota Twins
Plant City	Cincinnati Reds
Port Charlotte	Texas Rangers
Port St. Lucie	New York Mets
St. Petersburg	St. Louis Cardinals
Sarasota	Chicago White Sox
Vero Beach	Los Angeles Dodgers
West Palm Beach	Atlanta Braves and Montreal Expos
Winter Haven	Boston Red Sox

Florida is blessed with sunshine year-round. The warm Gulf Stream heats the air in winter and provides cool tropical breezes in summer. Temperatures range from 60° to 70° in the winter months (December to April) south of Orlando. It's usually 10° or 15° cooler north of Orlando. Even if you happen to hit a cool day, you can bet that it's warmer than those states north of Florida's border. Snow has been known to fall, but it's very rare and it never sticks.

Humid summer temperatures range between 80° and 90° throughout the state. In Florida, though, *everything* is air conditioned, so you can always find a place to cool off. Visitors often plan outdoor activities for the morning and late afternoon and avoid the noonday sun in an air-conditioned mall or restaurant.

Because Florida is closer to the equator than its northern neighbors, the sun here is more powerful, even on cloudy or overcast days. Protect yourself from a painful sunburn by using sunscreen lotion—and lots of common sense. It's better to be safe than sorry!

Did you know?

Florida has been given 3 nicknames: the Sunshine State, the Peninsula State, and the Everglade State.

Florida's hottest months also tend to be the wettest. Daily thunderstorms bring a welcome relief to the heat of June, July, and August. But the rain disappears as quickly as it comes, often leaving behind cool, clean air and a lovely rainbow.

June to November is the official hurricane season in Florida, although storms before August are rare. But this shouldn't keep you from planning a trip during these months. Today's weathermen can predict a storm far in advance, well before it reaches the Florida coastline. You'll have plenty of time to prepare for it or to leave the area.

Did you know?

When swirling winds reach 74 mph, they're classified as a hurricane. The storms can range from 60 miles to 1,000 miles in diameter and usually last from 8 to 10 days.

PACKING FOR THE TRIP

Leave your winter clothes, coats, and boots in your closet when packing for your trip—you won't need them. Instead, pack shorts, play clothes, bathing suits, and T-shirts, because not only is Florida warm, but dress is casual, too. A light jacket or sweater may be needed for winter nights, or a light raincoat and umbrella for summer showers.

Bring clothes that are cool and comfortable, and at least one pair of walking shoes or sneakers for the many miles you'll trek at Walt Disney World or Busch Gardens. You'll also want to bring a hat and sunscreen lotion to battle the sun's rays. And don't forget your camera. Who knows, you might even get to pose with Mickey Mouse!

T·R·A·V·E·L D·I·A·R·Y

We will be leaving _____ on _____
and arriving in _____ on _____.
We will travel by _____, and it should
take us about _____. We have to
_____ to get to Florida.
travel through _____.
Once we get there, we will stay at _____
We plan to visit all these places on our trip: _____
_____
_____
I am ____ hours/ ____ days/ ____ miles away from home.

GETTING THERE

Most everyone wants to visit Florida at one time or another, and getting there is really easy. Nearly every town has an airport, train station, bus station, and car rental companies—each trying to offer the best deal.

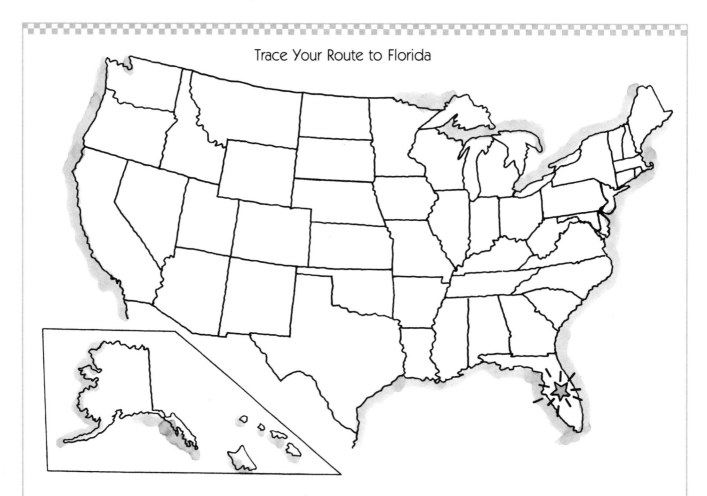

Trace Your Route to Florida

Whether by car, train, bus, or airplane, there was a route you had to follow to reach your destination. Color in the state where you live and draw a line tracing your path from home to vacation spot.

Isn't it exciting to know that you can climb aboard a giant silver bird and be in Florida the same day? If it's wintertime, you can get on the plane in the middle of a snowstorm and step off in the warm tropical sun. Fifty years ago visiting Florida wasn't so easy, but today air travel is quite common and convenient to all major cities.

Although not as many people travel to Florida by train as by car and airplane, it's certainly an alternative. If you have the extra time to spend, trains can be an interesting way to see the Florida peninsula, as well as all the states between your home and Florida. If your train ride is longer than 24 hours, you may want to get a slumber couch or roomette. This will give you a little more privacy and room to stretch out for a snooze.

Perhaps the best way to travel to Florida is by car. Pack a cooler full of drinks, sandwiches, and snacks and you're ready to go. Good roads and expressways make traveling easy. If you alternate drivers, you can be in sunny Florida in 24 to 26 hours from the Northeast or Midwest. And you won't have to lose a minute more of sun time.

GETTING AROUND

If you don't have your car with you, renting one while you're in Florida is a good idea. The places you'll want to visit are spread out, and although suitable bus and train transportation exists, you'll end up wasting a lot of time if you don't have your own wheels.

11

Florida is a very large state—500 miles from north to south, and as much as 400 miles from east to west (in the Panhandle region), although most of the peninsula runs 100 to 200 miles across. In fact, the state stretches over 2 time zones: eastern in most of the state, and central in a great part of the Panhandle.

Even without your own wheels, it may be possible to visit major attractions using courtesy buses provided by most of the major area hotels. In Orlando, for instance, courtesy buses could take you to Walt Disney's Magic Kingdom and to Sea World.

LET'S GET STARTED

Are you ready to step out into the magical world of Florida? It's a wonderland of nature and technology, a fine blend of relaxation and excitement. It's a land of white sand beaches and swaying palm trees, grassy inland "prairies" and cattle ranches, groves of citrus trees, and the impenetrable Everglades. You'll see strange plants and even stranger animals. And there's so much to do. You can play on the beach, explore museums, visit animals in the zoos, and zoom with speeding roller coasters. It's all waiting for you.

T·R·A·V·E·L D·I·A·R·Y

We're going to Florida in the _____ time. The weather is supposed to be _____, so I packed _____ to wear. I also brought _____, because I know I will need it/them to _____.

What I like best about vacations is _____

Of all the places I've heard about in Florida, I am most excited about seeing _____, because _____.

Was It Always Like This?

NATIVE AMERICANS

There were people living in Florida at least 12,000 years ago—so modern archaeologists tell us. They've pieced together some of the history and life-styles of the earliest residents by studying ancient tools and other artifacts found buried in Florida's soil.

Native Americans lived here long before Columbus discovered this new land. They fished, hunted, farmed, and fought among tribes for survival. When the white man invaded their land, they fought hard to protect what was theirs. But by 1765, most of the Indian population had died from war, enslavement, or disease.

Throughout the early history of Florida, many countries argued over possession of the land. The Spanish, British, French, American, and Native American peoples each put up a fight to control the peninsula. And the government passed back and forth many times.

Did you know?

Fossils of many prehistoric animals have been found in Florida, such as mammoths, saber-toothed tigers, and mastodons.

■ ■ ■

There are many Indian mounds in Florida and their contents are protected under the law. Do not ever remove material from one of these sites.

Speak and Spell

Many places in Florida are named with Indian words.

Name	Indian Meaning
Okeechobee	big water
Ocala	spring
Caloosa-hatchee	River of the Calu-sas
Apalachicola	Place of the Ruling People

UNDER SPANISH AND ENGLISH RULE

The Spanish explorer Ponce de León waded ashore near St. Augustine in 1513. He had come in search of gold and a rumored fountain of youth. He named the land *La Florida* in honor of Spain's Eastertime Feast of Flowers, *Pascua Florida.*

Ask your family to give you words to fill in the blanks. Under each blank is the part of speech needed to keep the sentence grammatical. When all the blanks are filled in, read the paragraph aloud. It'll be hysterical!

The Spanish _____ (occupation), Ponce de León, waded ashore near St. Augustine in 1513. He had come in search of _____ (plural noun) and a rumored _____ (noun). He named the land _____ (noun) in honor of _____ (holiday).

He returned again in 1521 and _____ (past-tense verb) on the southwestern coast near _____ (place). He was not welcomed by the _____ (plural noun) of this area, and fled to _____ (place), where he later _____ (past-tense verb) without finding his _____ (noun) or _____ (noun).

15

He returned again in 1521 and landed on the southwestern coast near Fort Myers. He was not welcomed by the Indians of this area and so fled to Cuba, where he later died without finding his gold or fountain of youth.

Three other Spaniards tried to establish claim to Florida between 1559 and 1561, but each was unsuccessful.

It wasn't until 1565 that Pedro Menéndez de Avilés succeeded in starting a colony in St. Augustine, which has become the oldest continuously settled site in the United States. It wasn't easy, however. First he had to get rid of the French, who had arrived just before him. And afterwards, he had to fight the British, who tried to step in. The battle for possession was on.

Raids and sieges riddled the years that followed, with settlements passing from Spain to England and back again. In 1763, England finally gained control of Florida in exchange for Havana, Cuba, which the English had captured from Spain during the Seven Years' War.

But trouble hadn't yet ended for Florida. Twenty years later, Spain regained Florida through the settlement that ended the American Revolution. But this would last only until 1821 when, after many border disputes, Spain agreed to sell Florida to the United States for $5 million.

THE SEMINOLE WARS

Americans began to move into Florida, and as the population increased, so did the pressure to rid the area of its Indians. An immigrant tribe of Creek Indians known as Seminoles had moved to Florida in the 1700s and controlled much of the land from Tallahassee to Lake Okeechobee. In 1818, General Andrew Jackson was sent into western Florida to push the tribe south, setting off the First Seminole War—a series of brief skirmishes involving a very small area. The Second Seminole War began when the Federal government tried to move the Seminoles onto a reservation in what is now Oklahoma. A young brave named Osceola plunged his knife into the white man's treaty, crying, "The only treaty I will ever make is this!" Inspired by Osceola's bravery, the Seminoles rebelled.

Did you know?

Tallahassee was chosen as Florida's capital city in 1824—when it was just a territory of the U.S.—and remains the seat of Florida government today.

Did you know?

Technically, the Seminoles are *still* at war with the United States today, since they never declared it over.

In 1837, after much fighting, Osceola rode into St. Augustine under a white flag of truce given to him by an American general. But the general had tricked the brave, and Osceola was imprisoned with his wives, children, and 116 others at Fort Moultrie in Charleston. The Seminole spirit was broken, and in 1858, after Chief Billy Bowlegs led the Third Seminole War, most of the Indians were moved to the reservation in Oklahoma. Some Seminoles managed to slip into the mysterious Everglades, however, where their descendants still live in harmony with nature.

STATEHOOD AND CIVIL WAR

Florida became the 27th state in 1845, but peace was still elusive. Slavery was a way of life in Florida, where the economy was based on agriculture and cotton plantations were important. Floridians could not understand why northerners sought to abolish slavery, and in 1861 Florida seceded from the Union. Civil war followed.

Although no major battles were fought on Florida soil, Florida sent troops and supplies to aid the Confederacy. In the end, Tallahassee was the only southern capital east of the Mississippi River to avoid capture during the war.

BEGINNING TO GROW

Before the Civil War, Florida had prospered, but the war stopped progress in its tracks. The trick was to get the state back on its feet and headed in the right direction. The railroad was just what Florida needed to boost trade and tourism.

Two millionaires, Henry Morrison Flagler and Henry B. Plant, built large hotels for the wealthy and raced to lay tracks down each coast with the hope of bringing northerners to vacation in the South. Flagler established a railroad down the eastern coast of Florida, stretching from Jacksonville all the way to Key West. Henry B. Plant's West Coast railroad reached from Richmond, Virginia, to Tampa. Land developers poured into the state and the boom was on.

History Crossword Puzzle

1. He discovered Florida in 1513.
2. Group of Creek Indians who controlled much of Florida in 1700s.
3. He said, "The only treaty I will ever make is this!"
4. This followed soon after Florida seceded from the Union.
5. This brought many people into Florida.
6. The U.S. purchased Florida from this country.
7. Ponce de León landed near here in 1521.
8. Florida grows a lot of this.
9. First name of the 2 millionaires who built large hotels for the wealthy.
10. Industry that brings billions of dollars into Florida every year.

(Answers on page 145)

But tourism wasn't the only industry to thrive. Many tourists never left the Sunshine State and the population soared. Cattle raising and the citrus industry took flight, and cigar manufacturing, sponge harvesting, and phosphate mining added to the state's growth. Cities sprang up along the railroad and farms were built in areas that were once swamplands.

But this development wasn't to last. In the late 1920s, the Great Depression, devastating hurricanes, and the invasion of the Mediterranean fruit fly shattered Florida's dreams of prosperity.

Fortunately, the state became a training center for military personnel during World War II, giving Florida a second chance.

FLORIDA TODAY

Today, Florida's economy is thriving. Tourism, real estate, citrus, and cattle bring in billions of dollars. And the people of Florida have a great deal to do with this growth.

Several immigrant groups have had a strong influence in the direction Florida has taken, from the Seminoles on reservations to the Greeks of Tarpon Springs to the Japanese of Delray Beach. A unique blend of people live here, all with their own reasons to make Florida home.

Since 1959, Cubans have been arriving in southern Florida in record numbers as they flee the communist government of Fidel Castro. Most have settled in Greater Miami. In fact, there's a small section in southwestern Miami known as Little Havana where Spanish is more widely spoken than English.

Did you know?

One out of every 5 Floridians is a senior citizen.

■ ■ ■

Over 30 million out-of-state visitors come to Florida each year, making tourism the largest industry in the state.

But when you think of Florida, senior citizens are sure to come to mind. Since the 1930s, retirees have flocked to the warm climate of Florida. Some are snowbirds, living in Florida during the winter (like birds that fly south), and returning north in summer. Others live here year-round. There are even condominium and mobile home complexes that cater exclusively to the elderly. You can usually pick out one of these places by the abundance of shuffleboard courts and giant tricycles.

Florida continues to grow. The 1960s saw the birth of the Kennedy Space Center at Cape Canaveral, where man continues to probe outer space. Walt Disney World opened its doors in 1971, revolutionizing the world of tourism. In 1982, it further transformed our ideas of entertainment with the $800-million EPCOT Center. Who knows how far Florida has yet to go? It's an ever-changing and growing state that you'll want to visit again and again.

T·R·A·V·E·L D·I·A·R·Y

People come to Florida from all over the world, both to live here and to visit. I come from _____.

My parents come from _____.

My ancestors come from _____.

Immigrant groups have had a strong influence in the history of Florida. I've seen people from many different countries on this trip. Some are from:

___ Canada   ___ China   ___ Puerto Rico
___ Japan   ___ Scotland   ___ England
___ Spain   ___ Italy   ___ Ireland
___ Mexico   ___ Greece   ___ Russia
___ France   ___ Cuba   _____

And I've heard some different languages spoken. Even the English some people speak here sounds different because of their accents. If I ever learn to speak another language, I will choose _____, because _____.

When Will We Eat?

So, you say you're hungry. You had better be *real* hungry, because there are many "specialties" in Florida.

Probably the most famous of all Florida foods is a tangy dessert called Key lime pie. It looks a lot like lemon meringue pie—with a graham cracker crust smothered in whipped cream or fluffy meringue—but has a more tart taste. Don't let anyone fool you with a pie made from ordinary limes. *Real* Key lime pie is yellow, not green.

Obviously fruit is a specialty in Florida. There aren't many places in the United States where you can walk into your backyard and pick a fresh grapefruit or an orange for breakfast. Most restaurants feature freshly squeezed juice. Take a trip to a citrus grove, where you can pick your own fruit. And if all that work makes you thirsty, some groves let you have all the orange juice you can drink—free! But don't just stick to grapefruit and oranges—try some unusual tropical fruits like mangoes, papayas, and sapodillas. Be daring!

Did you know?

Key West's small, yellow-colored limes originally came from Haiti and other Caribbean countries.

■ ■ ■

Florida is the world's largest citrus-producing region. It supplies 50 percent of the world's grapefruit, 25 percent of the world's oranges, and 95 percent of the country's limes.

■ ■ ■

Orange juice was made the official state beverage in 1967.

The Old South has had an influence on Florida cuisine. Some Florida restaurants will offer you a choice of home fries or grits with your breakfast. Grits taste and look just like their name. Mix them with milk and honey, or eat them hot with melted butter on top. That's the way most southerners like them.

Another Old South side dish that'll turn your fish into a feast are hush puppies, little cornmeal dumplings deep-fried until they're golden brown. Mmm . . . they're tasty!

No matter where you go in Florida, seafood tops the list of food favorites. After all, Florida is surrounded by water and loaded with lakes and rivers. This is your chance to try all kinds of fish and shellfish. Put on a bib, grab a stack of napkins, and dig your way through a whole platter of stone-crab claws. They're messy, but they're a treat well worth the fuss.

For something a little less messy but just as good, try pompano, a light and delicate fish often baked in a paper bag. Catfish, spotted sea trout, and Northern Florida mullet are other Florida favorites. Some popular shellfish are spiny lobster (crawfish), rock shrimp, scallops, clams, and oysters.

If you're in Key West, don't pass up a taste of conch chowder (pronounced *konk*), made from the creature that lives inside the pink shells you "listen to." The meat is a local delicacy and is usually served with Key lime and hot-pepper sauces.

Because so many people of different nationalities live in Florida, ethnic foods are very popular. For a taste of Cuba, try a Cuban restaurant in Miami's Little Havana or Tampa's Ybor City. There you can have *piccadillo*—a combination of ground meat, olives, and raisins—or *paella*—a tasty combination of yellow rice, seafood, and vegetables. Usually *pan Cubano*, a long crusty loaf of bread, will be served with your meal.

In Tarpon Springs, you can try an authentic Greek dish such as a big Greek salad or *moussaka*. You're not through eating, though, until you've had *baklava*, a sticky, sweet, and flaky treat.

There are many more ethnic restaurants—Chinese, Japanese, Italian, English, German, Spanish, Caribbean, Czechoslovakian, French, and even New York City deli! But don't be worried if you're not looking for a place where you have to sit down and relax while waiting for a waiter. Florida has all your favorite fast-food joints, and you know what's best on the menu there!

T·R·A·V·E·L D·I·A·R·Y

While in Florida, I want to try all these foods:

___Key lime pie   ___*piccadillo*   ___stone-crab claws

___*baklava*   ___catfish   ___hearts of palm

___mango   ___grits   ___mullet

___papaya   ___hush puppies   ___conch

My favorite food is _____. Of all the

food I tasted here in Florida, I liked _____the best.

Fun places I ate: What I ate there:

_____   _____

_____   _____

_____   _____

_____   _____

Do They Have Souvenirs?

No trip is complete without something to show your friends back home. It doesn't have to be expensive—it just has to be something you couldn't buy in your local mall. And it needs to remind you of the fun you've had in Florida.

Shopping is a favorite pastime in the Sunshine State. You'll come across street vendors, small gift shops, large department stores, flea markets, roadside stands, and futuristic shopping malls. Nearly every attraction you visit will have its own gift shop, and in the case of Walt Disney World, Busch Gardens, and Sea World, there are many shops where you can buy souvenirs to remind you of your trip long after you get home.

Take home a plastic flamingo, a can of sunshine, shell sculptures, keychains, and postcards—some of the stock items that can be found in most any shop. Maybe you want a bottle of water from St. Augustine's Fountain of Youth, a pair of Mickey Mouse ears from Walt Disney World, or a Shamu pool float from Sea World.

A really special souvenir—for yourself or for a friend back home—is a crate of Florida oranges or grapefruit. Most places will ship it for you at a small charge. If you carry it on the plane with you, make sure you mark your name on it clearly, because there are sure to be others bringing fruit home, too. You'd be very surprised if you got home with grapefruit when you bought oranges!

Probably the most popular souvenir is something you don't have to buy at all. You can pick it up right off the beach. Seashells make great souvenirs and gifts. Give them as is or make them into ashtrays, jewelry, or little sculptures. If you don't get a chance to do some beachcombing, you can always buy shells at the many shell shops along the coasts.

Did you know?

The larger citrus packers and shippers usually have much better prices than the specialty stores. Check with the shippers to make sure you're not violating a state law by bringing produce across a border.

T·H·E N·O·R·T·H·E·A·S·T C·O·A·S·T

The state of Florida was born in the northeast of the peninsula. First St. Augustine and then Jacksonville welcomed people to its shores. Today you'll find many reminders of Florida's colorful past in its buildings, street names, parks, and fortresses.

You'll immediately notice that the Northeast Coast is unlike the rest of Florida, where palm trees and glistening sand seem to stretch for miles. Here, the coast is much more rugged, with concrete-hard beaches perfect for driving on—and lots of people do just that—and giant oak trees and pines. It's as if the rest of the United States didn't quite know where to stop, nor Florida where to begin. It makes for a lovely combination of North and South.

29

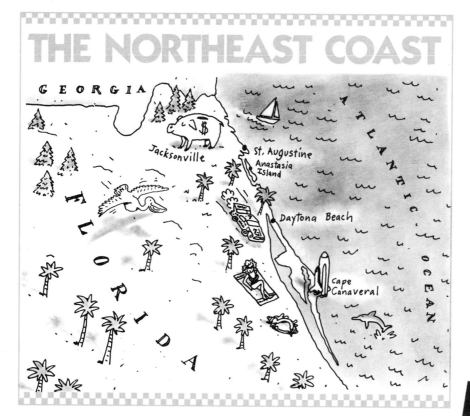

THE NORTHEAST COAST

GEORGIA

Jacksonville

St. Augustine
Anastasia
Island

FLORIDA

ATLANTIC OCEAN

Daytona Beach

Cape Canaveral

THE CITIES

Jacksonville is sometimes called the "Gateway to Florida." It's the first large city you'll come to when entering Florida from the East Coast. In fact, it's the largest city (in land area) in the continental United States.

Jacksonville—named for Andrew Jackson—sits on the banks of the St. Johns River. It's a bustling city with the flavor of the Old South and the sophistication of a major business district. Skyscrapers and old Southern homes blend to give Jacksonville a unique look. As in any city, and particularly a city in Florida, there's a lot here to see and do.

Did you know?

Jacksonville is Florida's banking and insurance center.

Did you know?

The St. Johns River is one of the few rivers in the United States that flow northward.

If history's your thing, Florida has a special place for you—an entire city brimming with history.

Today, **St. Augustine** is considered the first permanent settlement and the oldest city in the United States. Stepping into St. Augustine is like taking a trip back in time. Narrow cobblestone streets, coquina (pronounced *ko-KEE-nah*) homes, and horse-drawn carriages re-create life in America's Oldest City.

Every spring, thousands of college students flock to **Daytona Beach.** But spring isn't the only time things are fun here. Daytona calls itself the "World's Most Famous Beach"—and it just may be right. The 23 miles of hard-packed sparkling sand is perfect for sunning and swimming. A boardwalk lines the ocean along Main Street, where you'll find an amusement park, arcade, fishing pier, and sky ride.

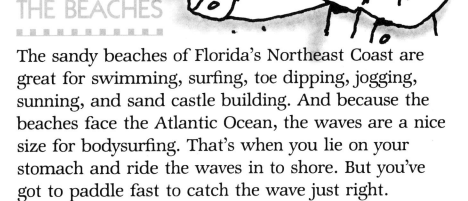

THE BEACHES

The sandy beaches of Florida's Northeast Coast are great for swimming, surfing, toe dipping, jogging, sunning, and sand castle building. And because the beaches face the Atlantic Ocean, the waves are a nice size for bodysurfing. That's when you lie on your stomach and ride the waves in to shore. But you've got to paddle fast to catch the wave just right.

What's That?

MUSEUM OF SCIENCE AND HISTORY

Bursting with exhibits, activities, and surprises, the Museum of Science and History is loved by kids and grown-ups alike! It's a delightful smorgasbord of hands-on exhibits that introduce the worlds of science, history, and nature. There's so much to do that you won't know where to go first—the Science PODS, the saltwater aquarium, the model of the Dent Mound archaeological site, the planetarium. It's educational, but more than that, it's fun!

FORT CAROLINE

Fort Caroline was established about 5 miles from the mouth of the St. Johns River in 1564 by Huguenots (French Protestants). Had the Fort Caroline settlement survived, it would have been the oldest town in the United States. Many battles were fought here by both white men and red, Spanish and French. The original fortress was washed away sometime after 1880 when

Did you know?

Fort Caroline National Memorial is the site of the first clash between European powers—France and Spain.

The fort was rebuilt according to 16th-century sketches by Jacques Le Moyne, the colony's artist and mapmaker.

T·R·A·V·E·L D·I·A·R·Y

Of all the places we visited on the Northeast Coast of Florida, I liked _____ the best. That's because _____. I wanted to see _____, but we didn't have a chance to go there. Maybe next time.

❖ ❖ ❖

the river channel was deepened. But the fort's walls have been reconstructed on the river plain to look just as they originally did.

HISTORICAL ST. AUGUSTINE

The best way to see St. Augustine is on foot, but before you step out on your own, take a narrated tour of the city on one of the sight-seeing trains or horse-drawn carriages. You'll bump over cobblestone streets as the guide points out the sights and tells some interesting tales to go with them.

Did you know?

At the St. Augustine Visitors Information and Preview Center, you can see a 28-minute film about the city and pick up brochures and information on attractions and events.

▪ ▪ ▪

Two exciting films provide a fascinating introduction to America's Oldest City. You can see them at the new Museum-Theater, one block from the Old City Gates.

Castillo de San Marcos National Monument proudly stands guard over the city. This fort, begun in 1672, was constructed by the Spanish to protect themselves against English invaders. The 16-foot-thick coquina walls surrounded by a 40-foot-wide moat have held strong against enemy cannonballs and the weather of hundreds of years.

Did you know?

The iron chain placed around the oldest schoolhouse was put there to keep the building from flying away in the event of a hurricane. It seems it worked!

St. George Street, across from the fort, is lined with restored 18th-century Spanish houses. This area is called the **Old Spanish Quarter.** Here you can see demonstrations by a blacksmith, leather worker, and printer; homes dating back several hundred years; and the country's oldest schoolhouse. Nestled in among the history are wonderful gift shops, perfect for browsing or finding just the right souvenir.

Over on St. Francis Street is the **Oldest House,** also known as the Gonzales-Alvarez House. It was built of coquina and wood in the early 1700s. The home is restored much as it was in its historic past. A museum, ornamental gardens, and a research library are on the grounds.

What's Wrong with This Picture?

(Answers on page 145)

Packed into the **Oldest Store Museum** are antiques of every kind. Bright red underwear, laced-up corsets, high-buttoned shoes, toys, butter churns, groceries, and chamber pots line the walls and floors of this turn-of-the-century general store. Back in the 1800s, this store was the hub of St. Augustine's social, political, and economic life. People would gather here to catch up on the latest news while shopping, getting a tooth pulled, having spectacles fitted, or even getting a haircut!

If you see a large, red, unusual-looking building that doesn't seem to fit with the rest of the town, chances are it's **Zorayda Castle.** This castle was built in 1883 by eccentric Boston millionaire Franklin Smith. It's a replica (1/10 the size) of Spain's famous Moorish palace, Alhambra. The main attraction here is a 2,300-year-old rug made out of Egyptian cat hair. It was found wrapped with a mummy.

Word Scramble

The letters in the words below are all mixed up. Can you unscramble them?

dorazya talesc _____   grilenth semuum _____

lapklrab somerime _____   storept axw mumsue _____

nitfaonu fo thyou _____   dol painshs uterraq _____

listloca ed ans cromas _____   steldo resto smuume _____

(Answers on page 145)

Next door to this unusual structure you'll find the **Lightner Museum,** housed in the former Alcazar Hotel built by Henry Morrison Flagler in 1883. The museum contains a large collection of 19th-century furnishings, costumes, toys, and decorative art. Across the street is the most elaborate and luxurious hotel built by Henry Morrison Flagler, the Ponce de León. Today it houses Flagler College.

If the word *diamond* makes you think of green grass, freshly roasted peanuts, and hot dogs, you won't want to pass up a tour of **Ballpark Memories,** a baseball museum filled with relics from the golden years of America's favorite sport. You'll see some rare baseball cards, uniforms worn by the stars of yesterday, and great action photos. Collectors can purchase baseball cards, programs, and photographs in the store attached to the museum.

Have your picture taken with one of history's greats. At **Potter's Wax Museum** over 150 historical figures come to life under the careful hand of leading European artists. And the exciting video displays and multi-image theater presentation there will impress the most unimpressed.

Did you know?

You can see the craftsmen at work in the Wax Works.

If you're a fan of the odd, weird, and unusual, St. Augustine has a museum for you! Over 750 oddities—including a shrunken head, a two-headed calf, and a log cabin replica made out of 16,360 Lincoln pennies—are on display at **Ripley's Believe It or Not Museum**. It's one of the strangest museums you'll ever see—believe it or not!

For those of you who don't want to grow up, take a drink from the **Fountain of Youth**. In 1513, Ponce de León waded ashore here and recorded the discovery of North America. The actual stone marker he laid is still in place. And if your drink hasn't sent you back to infancy, don't miss the celestial navigation show in the planetarium. Here you'll see just what the sky looked like on the night before Ponce de León set foot on the banks of North America. These same stars guided him across the vast ocean and to the New World.

Did you know?

Over 400 years ago, Father Lopez de Mendoza Grajales offered the first mass in America's first city at the Mission of Nombre de Dios. This was the beginning of Christianity in the United States. A 208-foot-tall metal cross marks the spot.

37

Did you know?

NASA has launched all of America's manned space flights from Kennedy Space Center.

Can you name the planets in our solar system starting from the one closest to the sun? Hint: There are 9 of them.

_____

_____

_____

_____

_____

_____

_____

_____

_____

(Answers on page 145)

CAPE CANAVERAL

Enter **Spaceport USA** at Kennedy Space Center for an adventure into the world of astronauts and space exploration. Begin your tour at the Visitors Center, where you'll see huge rockets and spacecraft, space flight demonstrations, hands-on displays, and interesting films. A 2-hour National Aeronautics and Space Administration (NASA) escorted bus tour takes you on a fascinating trip through the astronaut training building, simulators, and the 52-story Vehicle Assembly Building, where the space vehicles are put together. You'll also visit Mission Control Center and Launch Pads 39A and 39B, where the early moon-bound flights were launched. Don't miss the exciting 20-minute film in the IMAX Theater depicting the launch and landing of the space shuttle *Columbia*.

Are There Any Animals?

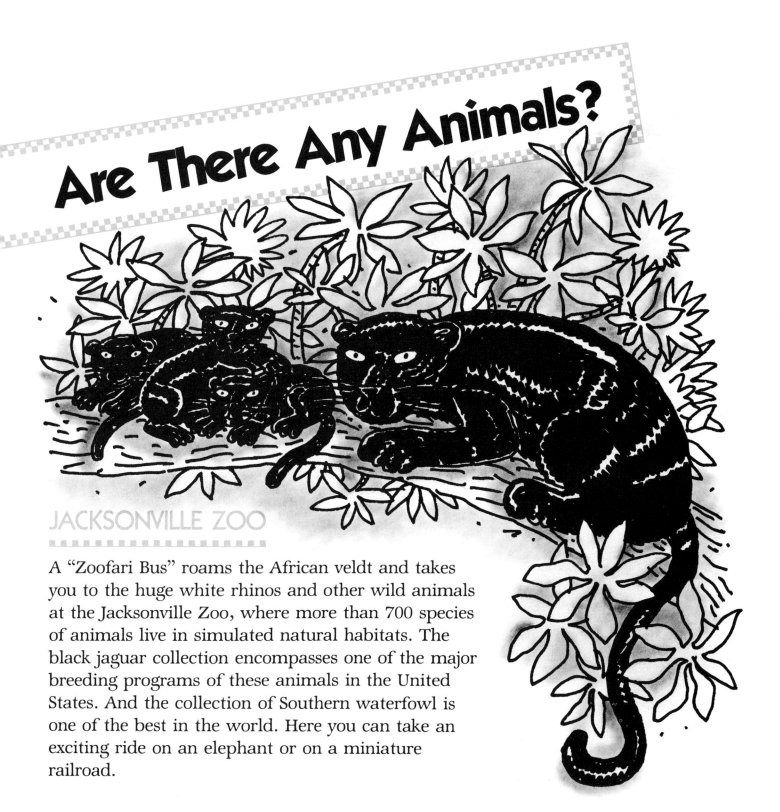

JACKSONVILLE ZOO

A "Zoofari Bus" roams the African veldt and takes you to the huge white rhinos and other wild animals at the Jacksonville Zoo, where more than 700 species of animals live in simulated natural habitats. The black jaguar collection encompasses one of the major breeding programs of these animals in the United States. And the collection of Southern waterfowl is one of the best in the world. Here you can take an exciting ride on an elephant or on a miniature railroad.

ST. AUGUSTINE ALLIGATOR FARM

Across the Bridge of Lions on Anastasia Island is the St. Augustine Alligator Farm, founded in 1893. Here you can see ostriches, snakes, giant tortoises, birds, monkeys, and of course, alligators. Explore Florida's wilds on an elevated walkway over a lagoon inhabited by menacing alligators. Many exciting presentations will keep you entertained, including an alligator wrestling show.

MARINELAND OF FLORIDA

Further along the coast you'll come to Marineland of Florida, the world's oldest oceanarium. Here you'll delight in seeing jumping dolphins, sea lions, penguins, and otters. Huge oceanariums are home to hundreds of species of marine life, and the 11 shows will keep you clapping.

C·E·N·T·R·A·L F·L·O·R·I·D·A

Central Florida has more major attractions than any other part of the state. In fact, there are more fun things to do in the Orlando area than just about anywhere in the world! Before the appearance of Walt Disney World in 1971, this region was mostly orange groves and cattle ranches. Mickey Mouse sure changed that! There are still some citrus farms and agricultural areas, but it's the tourist attractions that bring millions of people to Central Florida today.

THE CITIES

Orlando is at the center of this tourism mecca, but the attractions extend far beyond its borders. Kissimmee, St. Cloud, Lake Wales, Haines City, Clermont, Ocala, and Winter Park radiate out from Orlando like spokes of a wheel, each with its own promises for fun and excitement.

You'll find so much adventure here that you'll barely have the strength to blink each night as you stumble into bed to rest up for the next day's delights. Whether it's animals, nature, museums, or theme parks you like, Orlando has them all!

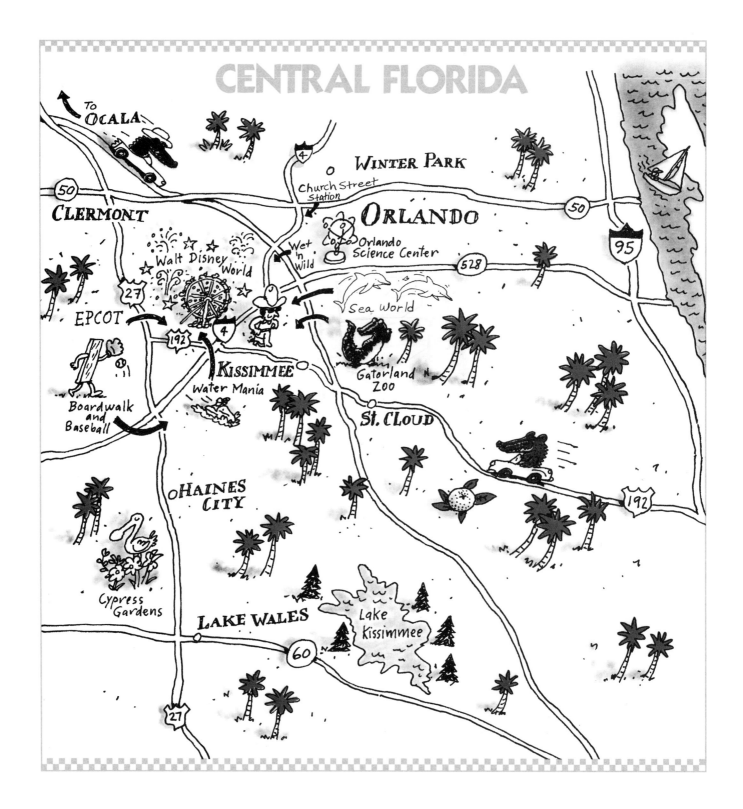

What's That?

ORLANDO SCIENCE CENTER

You'll love the hands-on science exhibits at Orlando Science Center. These special exhibits display different principles in ways that make science fun. There's also a Discovery Room just for kids and a planetarium that stages shows on space during the day and elaborate laser light shows on weekend evenings. Don't you wish science could be this much fun at school?

XANADU

For a most unusual attraction, visit Xanadu, a home of tomorrow. This futuristic white bubble is what life in the 21st century may be like. There's a waterfall/spa in the master bedroom, a solar-heated sauna, an indoor pool, and a greenhouse. In the Learning Center, you can watch the "house brain" control the interior environment and see the computer-voice command center. Best of all is the robot butler who helps direct you through this amazing showplace.

CHURCH STREET STATION

For a rip-roarin' good time, head for Church Street Station, a lively complex of eating and drinking establishments where entertainment is the main course. The most popular restaurant here is **Rosie O'Grady's Good Time Emporium,** where you'll be entertained with Dixieland music and high-stepping cancan dancers. If you've spent any time on the beach, you're sure to have seen the airplanes pulling banners advertising this place. **Apple Annie's Courtyard** next door is a grand Victorian garden with bluegrass and folk music, and **Phineas Phogg's Balloon Works** is a lively disco. For a quiet break from the fast pace, try **Lili Marlene's Aviators Pub and Restaurant,** where you'll be surrounded by the history of aviation. Across the street is **Cheyenne Saloon and Opera House,** an ornate establishment that looks like the Grand Ole Opry House in Nashville, Tennessee. Here you'll see clogging exhibitions, listen to country music, and eat barbecue style. And don't miss the **Church Street Exchange,** a new 3-level shopping area.

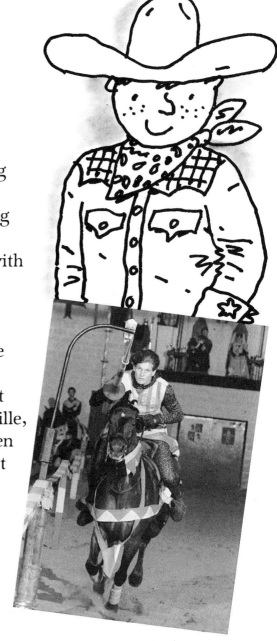

Did you know?

Eating with your fingers is allowed here. They don't even give you any silverware!

DINNER SHOWS

Within an 11th-century European castle is a very special dining experience. **Medieval Times Dinner and Tournament** combines a 4-course feast with authentic jousting matches and tournament games.

44

Did you know?

Glenn Randall, director of training at Arabian Nights, trained Trigger and the Black Stallion.

■ ■ ■

The Florida Citrus Tower in Clermont is the highest observation deck in Florida. It looks out over 2,000 square miles of rolling hills and citrus trees.

As you cross the drawbridge, you'll be greeted by the count and countess and presented with a crown. From there you'll be directed to your dining section, where you can cheer the brave knight on horseback whose costume is the same color as your crown. It's exciting, fast-paced fun. And the food's great.

A 5-course Western banquet is served up at **Fort Liberty.** This authentic stockade fort includes a trading post for specialty shopping, country music, and lots of Wild West entertainment. So put on your cowboy boots and get your taste buds ready!

If you like horses, you'll love **Arabian Nights,** a dinner theater where 60 horses perform in a 2½-acre Arabian-styled palace. The world-famous Lipizzans, Arabian "Dancing Horses of the Desert" (that's *desert*, not *dessert!*), Quarter Horses, American Saddlebreds, and Walter Farley's Black Stallion perform in a spectacular 2-hour show while you dine on a sumptuous 4-course dinner.

SPOOK HILL

Don't miss Spook Hill in Lake Wales—it's one of the craziest sights you'll ever see. Drive to 5th Street and stop at the bottom of the steep drive. Ask Mom or Dad to turn off the motor, put the car in neutral, and step off the brake. Then watch your car slowly roll backward . . . uphill!

WINTER PARK SINKHOLE

Winter Park, east of Orlando, is known for a very unusual attraction that draws hundreds of curious visitors. In 1981, a sinkhole opened up in the middle of town, swallowing 6 cars, an auto shop, a house, parts of 2 streets, and the deep end of the local public swimming pool. When it stopped sinking, it was almost 350 feet across, 100 feet deep, and it had eaten 2½ acres! You won't believe it until you see it!

Did you know?

Most of Florida's lakes started out as sinkholes.

OCALA NATIONAL FOREST

An hour's drive from Orlando, you can experience the breathtaking beauty of Ocala National Forest, a tremendous wonderland of nature. Nearly 400,000 acres of wilderness are open for exploration, by land or by water. A hiking trail runs the entire length of the forest—more than 66 miles! And Alexander and Juniper springs are just right for a day of canoeing, tubing, snorkeling, or just plain swimming.

Are There Any Animals?

Did you know?

Shamu Stadium holds 6 million gallons of water and has a performing pool that's 36 feet deep. It's the largest single-species research and display facility in the world.

■ ■ ■

Baby Shamu was born on September 26, 1985 in Shamu Stadium. She weighed 350 pounds and was 6 feet long!

SEA WORLD®

There's a place in Florida where you can feed a dolphin, pet a ray, or get doused by a killer whale. And where's that? Sea World®. There's no place like it.

You'll marvel at the grace and gentleness of 5-ton Shamu®, the killer whale, as he catapults through the air and plays games with his trainer. But beware: They're not kidding when they say you'll get wet if you sit in the first few rows. Even Baby Shamu®, the first killer whale ever to be born and thrive in the care of man, makes a grand appearance in the show.

But don't stop there. Sea World's "Sharks!" brings you face-to-face—through a thick plate of clear acrylic, of course—with fearsome sharks. A people mover transports you through a tunnel while these fearsome animals swim all around you.

Penguin Encounter is home to more than 200 tuxedoed birds living in a world of ice and snow. You'll giggle at these funny seabirds slipping and sliding on the rocks. They may waddle on the ground, but they're graceful swimmers.

Don't skip a visit to Sea Lions of the Silver Screen, where you'll see sea lions, otters, and even a walrus re-enact Hollywood's greatest classics. There are many more thrilling shows and exhibits that will keep you entertained.

For a break from the animals, visit Cap 'N Kids World, an unusual playground of surprises. "Swim" in a tank full of plastic balls, or climb a 55-foot pirate ship. You'll laugh your head off!

After a long day of sun and excitement, you may want to stop in at Places of Learning, a giant bookstore filled with books and educational materials just for kids. Outside the store is a giant 1-acre map of the United States surrounded by the state flags. You can walk around the states, crossing rivers, lakes, and cities with each step. See if you can find the city where you live. It's a full day of fun!

GATORLAND ZOO

There's a place in Kissimmee where you can hand-feed an alligator, handle a boa constrictor, or sample gator meat. Gatorland Zoo is home to over 5,000 alligators and crocodiles in their natural habitats, as well as to snakes, monkeys, zebras, bears, and birds.

Trained alligators leap high out of the water for food suspended from a cable 4 to 5 feet above the water

during the Gator Jumparoo show. You'll marvel at the training of these huge reptiles who respond to their own names.

Stroll a covered bridge and a 2,000-foot walkway through the cypress swamp, where you can study these enormous reptiles up close. They're practically right under your feet! Peer into a pit of deadly snakes. Or sit on Albert, a 300-pound tortoise from the Galapagos Islands. A trip to Gatorland Zoo is an unusual and exciting experience.

Kooky Questions

Q: What did the alligator say when the tourist stepped on his tail?

A: Nothing. Alligators can't talk.

REPTILE WORLD SERPENTARIUM

More than 60 varieties of reptiles can be found at Reptile World Serpentarium. Originally the serpentarium was a research center for the production and distribution of snake venoms, but now it offers guests a close-up view of cobras, pythons, rattlesnakes, lizards, turtles, and alligators.

CENTRAL FLORIDA ZOOLOGICAL PARK

More than 200 wild and exotic animals call the Central Florida Zoological Park in Sanford home. Many of the animals here are endangered species, and this may be your only chance to see some of them. There's also a petting zoo, pony rides, animal feeding demonstrations, and an elevated nature trail that winds through a swamp. This is a fairly small zoo, but that's what makes it so delightful.

Word Search

```
A  C  Y  P  R  E  S  S  G  A  R  D  E  N  S  E  A  W  O  R  L  D
O  G  E  W  T  Y  P  H  O  O  N  L  A  G  O  O  N  I  F  I  C  M
M  H  P  V  L  W  D  B  K  P  O  E  U  Q  U  Y  B  N  J  Z  E  E
F  I  C  H  U  R  C  H  S  T  R  E  E  T  S  T  A  T  I  O  N  D
T  E  O  X  U  N  F  O  R  T  L  I  B  E  R  T  Y  E  S  N  T  I
W  A  T  E  R  M  A  N  I  A  A  B  J  Z  O  P  R  R  W  Y  R  E
S  U  C  V  C  D  C  A  H  C  N  T  Q  J  L  M  I  P  E  H  A  V
I  N  E  G  P  G  M  R  O  R  D  M  O  W  N  A  A  A  T  T  L  A
L  I  N  A  S  W  N  X  C  D  O  W  K  C  Z  G  B  R  N  Y  F  L
V  V  T  T  J  I  G  W  A  X  S  D  V  E  R  I  M  K  W  A  L  T
E  E  E  O  R  L  Y  U  D  L  C  R  S  O  F  C  U  S  I  Z  O  I
R  R  R  R  H  D  C  Z  E  O  I  S  P  O  O  K  H  I  L  L  R  M
S  S  I  L  X  W  S  Q  K  V  E  J  E  P  L  I  K  N  D  Q  I  E
P  A  X  A  N  A  D  U  K  T  N  I  T  N  V  N  A  K  U  Y  D  S
R  L  W  N  D  T  G  B  A  B  C  S  M  Z  E  G  H  H  W  M  A  X
I  S  N  D  C  E  D  I  S  N  E  Y  M  G  M  D  G  O  R  W  Z  O
N  T  D  Z  O  R  Z  X  A  F  C  L  G  Q  F  O  V  L  D  L  O  E
G  U  A  O  Y  S  Q  P  M  M  E  R  F  A  O  M  N  E  H  K  O  G
S  D  I  O  A  R  A  B  I  A  N  N  I  G  H  T  S  G  V  H  B  N
Z  I  R  J  E  P  L  R  E  P  T  I  L  E  W  O  R  L  D  P  Z  C
L  O  W  A  L  T  D  I  S  N  E  Y  W  O  R  L  D  Q  F  W  L  T
F  S  N  Q  T  M  Y  S  L  E  R  Y  R  U  N  H  A  U  S  E  C  U
S  M  J  Y  O  K  L  A  N  I  O  M  J  K  L  E  F  Z  R  T  T  U
B  O  A  R  D  W  A  L  K  A  N  D  B  A  S  E  B  A  L  L  U  I
```

Xanadu	Reptile World	Cypress Gardens
Orlando Science Center	Central Florida Zoo	Boardwalk and Baseball
Church Street Station	Walt Disney World	Silver Springs
Winter Park Sinkhole	Magic Kingdom	Wild Waters
Spook Hill	EPCOT Center	Fort Liberty
Sea World	Water Mania	Medieval Times
Gatorland Zoo	Universal Studios	Arabian Nights
Disney/MGM	Wet 'n Wild	Typhoon Lagoon

(Answers on page 146)

Are We Having Fun Yet?

WALT DISNEY WORLD

There's no doubt that if you've come to Orlando, you plan to pay a visit to the world's most famous rodent, Mickey Mouse. He makes his home in Walt Disney World, which includes the Magic Kingdom, EPCOT Center, Walt Disney World Village, Fort Wilderness Campground, River Country, Discovery Island, Typhoon Lagoon, Pleasure Island, and Disney/MGM Studios. That's a lot of real estate for a little mouse. But Mickey isn't just *any* mouse now, is he?

Did you know?

Walt Disney World occupies 27,400 acres. Of that, the Magic Kingdom has 98 acres and EPCOT Center, 260 acres.

■ ■ ■

Walt Disney World is the largest tourist attraction in the world! There are as many as 80,000 people in the park on a busy day.

THE MAGIC KINGDOM

The Magic Kingdom is divided into 6 "lands": Main Street, U.S.A.; Adventureland; Frontierland; Liberty Square; Fantasyland; and Tomorrowland.

When you enter the park, you'll find yourself on Main Street, U.S.A., a turn-of-the-century American town where you can see what stores looked like around the year 1900.

Did you know?

Steamboat Willie, featured at Main Street Cinema, was the first sound cartoon and the film debut of Mickey Mouse.

■ ■ ■

Mickey was originally going to be named Mortimer, but Mrs. Disney convinced Walt to change it.

Did you know?

The ancient look of the Haunted Mansion requires lots of dust. This is purchased by the 5-pound bag and spread around haphazardly. A liquid is transformed into cobwebs by a secret process.

In Adventureland, visit a tropical paradise, complete with sights, sounds, and smells. Here you can climb the Swiss Family Island Treehouse, the ultimate in banyan-tree living. Or sail to adventure with the Pirates of the Caribbean and witness a spooky pirate raid.

In Frontierland, a foot-stomping good time awaits you at the Country Bear Vacation Hoedown, where singing bears and woodland creatures entertain you with down-home country and western songs.

If you like spooky houses, Liberty Square's Haunted Mansion is something you won't want to miss. Don't worry if you scare easily, there's more humor and special effects in this ghostly house than terror. Nearby is the Hall of Presidents, where you'll see our American presidents, past and present, and hear an address by Abraham Lincoln, courtesy of electronic wizardry!

Fantasyland, which includes Cinderella's castle, is often called "the happiest land of all." This is where your favorite fairy tales come to life. Don't miss It's A Small World, where children dressed in native costume sing of peace and brotherhood. The melody will run through your mind for hours. And if you keep your ears open, you're bound to hear others humming the tune as they stroll through the park.

Did you know?

The Magic Kingdom is actually the 2nd floor of the Disney complex. There are 1½ miles of underground tunnels where the attractions are controlled and coordinated.

■ ■ ■

Many of the park's shrubs are trimmed in the shape of animals. Can you figure out what each of them is?

Did you know?

EPCOT stands for *experimental prototype community of tomorrow*.

Can you name the 7 dwarfs from *Snow White and the Seven Dwarfs*?

—————————————
—————————————
—————————————
—————————————
—————————————
—————————————
—————————————

(Answers on page 146)

The future becomes the present in Tomorrowland, where a space-age roller coaster hurtles you through the outer reaches of space. It's an exciting— even scary—journey.

Special parades and shows can be seen daily throughout the park. Be sure to check the times and locations when you first arrive so you don't miss a thing.

EPCOT CENTER

You'll find 2 entertainment worlds at EPCOT Center—Future World and World Showcase. Together they make up an exciting theme park of their own that's like a super world's fair.

The Future World pavilions take a fascinating view of space, transportation, energy, and communication through hands-on games and informative films. Touch-sensitive video screens and computers give you the chance to experience new technology and experiment with their concepts. It may sound too educational to be fun, but that couldn't be further from the truth.

Take a ride through a Caribbean coral reef, test your skill and knowledge at video screens, and converse with a robot. You'll love the Image Works, a futuristic playground beyond your wildest imagination. Each of the 9 pavilions has oodles of activities to keep you entranced.

World Showcase celebrates the nations of the world through architecture, cuisine, souvenirs, and entertainment. Visit a lively Mexican plaza at dusk, journey through a mythical Norwegian forest aboard a dragon-headed Viking longboat, and witness the beauties of China and Canada in Circle Vision 360 films. These are just a few of the adventures in store at World Showcase. And you don't even need a passport!

Don't leave EPCOT Center early if "Illuminations" is on the evening's program. It's an amazing, spectacular, awe-inspiring display of lasers, fireworks, and dancing fountains put to music.

There's much more to Walt Disney World than the Magic Kingdom and EPCOT Center. Walt Disney World has recently added 2 new attractions. A 50-acre water park, **Typhoon Lagoon**, offers thrilling, fast-paced, splashing fun. Here you can surf 6½-foot

Test Your Disney Knowledge

1. Where in the Magic Kingdom can you find rides named after storybooks? _____ _____

2. What are the names of the 6 different "lands" in the Magic Kingdom? _____ _____ _____

3. Name 5 Disney animated movies. _____ _____ _____

4. What are the names of the 2 different sections of EPCOT Center? _____ _____

5. What do the letters in *EPCOT* stand for? _____ _____

(Answers on page 146)

waves, slip and slide down a twisty water chute, or swing from a vine and drop into a gushing waterfall.

Another exciting new attraction is **Disney/MGM Studios,** where you can tour a working television and motion picture production facility. Explore the back lots, the soundstages, and the animation department. You can even volunteer for a role in the Video Theater.

Now you can see why it's called Walt Disney World. It's an entire *world* of places to see. And there's so much to do, you'll never be bored!

T·R·A·V·E·L D·I·A·R·Y

I _____ Walt Disney World! We went to _____ and I saw _____. My favorite thing at Walt Disney World was _____, because _____. If I come back here, I want to _____.

❖ ❖ ❖

WATER MANIA

For a day of splashing good fun, head for Water Mania, where you can plummet down a 72-foot flume, surf the whitecaps, and spiral through a twisting slide. If all of this water has you looking like a prune, take a break for a picnic under the pines, a rest on the beach, or an exciting game of volleyball.

UNIVERSAL STUDIOS FLORIDA

There's a new motion picture entertainment attraction and studio facility in the Sunshine State. Universal Studios Florida will give you a behind-the-scenes look at how motion picture and television shows are made in a real working studio. Tour the back lots, visit a soundstage, and journey through the magical world of animation. It's a great chance to glimpse the world of "Hollywood" make-believe!

WET 'N WILD

Splash, slide, or bellyflop at Wet 'n Wild, a 25-acre water park where the slides are high and fast. Grab a tube and bump along the churning waters of Raging Rapids. Or hurtle down the twisting 7-story-tall Mach 5. You never knew that getting wet could be this much fun!

CYPRESS GARDENS

A trip to Cypress Gardens, Florida's Original

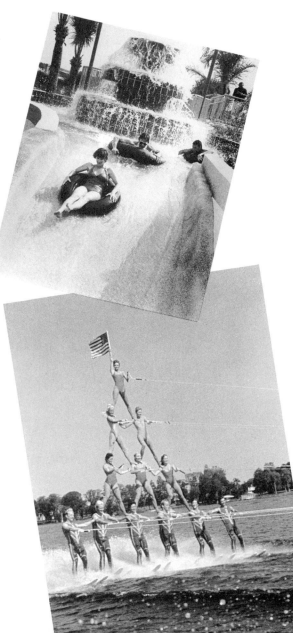

56

Showcase™, is like stepping into a garden paradise. Southern belles in hoopskirts stroll the paths and walkways that wind among colorful flowers, tall cypresses, and beautifully manicured lawns. Take the slowest ride of your life on a giant tortoise, pet a white-tailed deer, or spy on a tiny prairie dog. There's even a special nursery where you can see baby animals being cared for.

You can walk through an aviary teeming with toucans, and learn about Florida's alligators at the Gator Handling Demonstration. And don't miss the water-ski shows where athletes ski barefoot, backward, and over jumps. Nowhere else will you see such an amazing display of this water sport. Cypress Gardens is known as "the Water Ski Capital of the World."

Did you know?

The Australian emus' biological clocks keep Australian time—they lay their eggs in our fall, when it's spring "down under."

■ ■ ■

Esther Williams filmed underwater music spectaculars here in the 1950s.

■ ■ ■

"Southern Ice," a great skating revue with award-winning skaters, is the only permanent themed ice skating show in the Southeast.

Gulliver fell asleep in the garden, and while he was sleeping the plants grew. Can you help him find his way out?

(Answers on page 146)

BOARDWALK AND BASEBALL

Two of America's favorite pastimes are combined in Florida's newest theme park, Boardwalk and Baseball. A mile-long boardwalk connects the entire park, flanked by thrill rides, live entertainment, and a midway. Six major league–size playing fields host daily amateur baseball games. And during the spring, the Kansas City Royals train here.

Seventeen twisting curves will leave you breathless on the Grand Rapids log flume. And the 16-story-high Ferris wheel is one of the biggest in the world. Take a break from the rides and try your skill in one of the

T·R·A·V·E·L D·I·A·R·Y

There's so much to do in Central Florida that it's impossible to do it all. I got to go to _____, but I didn't get a chance to see _____. My favorite part about this area is _____ because _____. Some other things that I like are _____.

❖ ❖ ❖

batting cages or pitching machines, or try to win a prize at one of the many midway games. If you're an armchair athlete, watch a game on one of the playing fields or visit A Taste of Cooperstown, an official display of the National Baseball Hall of Fame and Museum.

SILVER SPRINGS

Just east of Ocala is the beautiful nature preserve of Silver Springs. Geologists believe there has been human activity at this spring for 100,000 years.

The best way to explore the clear waters of Silver Springs is aboard a glass-bottom boat. Hundreds of fish swim by below your feet—and they look so close that you'll want to reach out and touch them. Or take a jungle cruise that brings you within steps of the wild animals that live here.

At Deer Park, you can pet a baby giraffe and feed a white-tailed deer. And the smaller animals are just right for cuddling.

WILD WATERS

Right next door to Silver Springs is a 6-acre water theme part where you can splash to your heart's content. Race a friend down the 220-foot-long lightning-fast Silver Bullet, or shoot down the 400-foot-long Hurricane that winds through a tunnel before spitting you out into a bubbling pool. If you need a rest, there's a picnic area, snack bars, and even a miniature golf course for "drying-off" fun.

59

T·H·E S·O·U·T·H·E·A·S·T C·O·A·S·T

When you hear people speak of Southeast Florida, they're usually referring to the area beginning just north of the Palm Beaches—Palm Beach and West Palm Beach—and finishing up south of Miami, where the mainland meets the Florida Keys.

THE CITIES

The Palm Beaches sit at the northern edges of Southeast Florida. The most famous town here is beautiful **Palm Beach,** home to the wealthiest of the wealthy. Don't be surprised if you see multimillion-dollar homes, Rolls-Royces at every turn, and jewelry costing more than your house glittering from Worth Avenue shop windows.

Did you know?

It's against the law in Palm Beach to jog without a shirt on, to park almost anywhere, to own a kangaroo, or to hang a clothesline.

■ ■ ■

To find out who partied where and with whom, pick up a copy of the *Palm Beach Daily News.* And don't worry about getting newsprint on yourself, the paper here is treated to keep the ink from coming off on hands or clothes.

■ ■ ■

West Palm Beach is the headquarters for the Professional Golfers' Association (PGA).

60

THE SOUTHEAST COAST

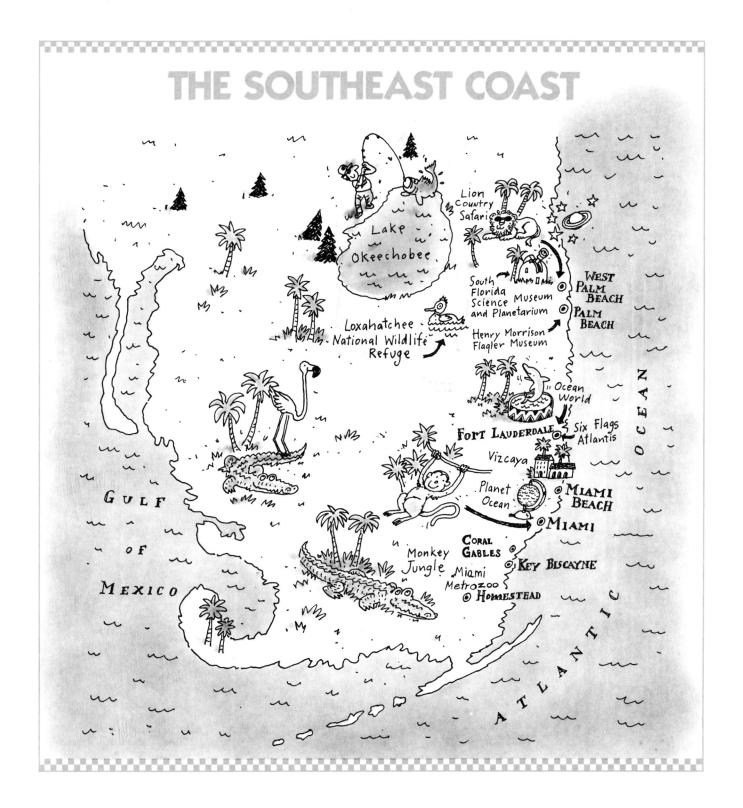

Lake Okeechobee

Lion Country Safari

South Florida Science Museum and Planetarium

WEST PALM BEACH

PALM BEACH

Loxahatchee National Wildlife Refuge

Henry Morrison Flagler Museum

Ocean World

FORT LAUDERDALE

Six Flags Atlantis

Vizcaya

Planet Ocean

MIAMI BEACH

MIAMI

CORAL GABLES

Monkey Jungle

KEY BISCAYNE

Miami Metrozoo

HOMESTEAD

GULF OF MEXICO

ATLANTIC OCEAN

Gulliver has gone to the beach for a day of fun in the sun, but some things are missing. Complete the picture.

West Palm Beach, on the other side of Lake Worth, is a large, modern city. It was originally created for house servants and others who worked for the Palm Beach wealthy. Today it's a thriving city and the commercial center for the forests of sugarcane that grow in much of Palm Beach County. If you get a chance, try sucking the sap of the cane. It's sweet!

South of the Palm Beaches is **Fort Lauderdale,** most famous as a beach resort. Its golden sand welcomes visitors year after year to come play in the clear waters.

Miami is a relatively new city. It got its start in the 1920s and 1930s and has already weathered some tough times, such as yellow-fever epidemics, fires, and severe hurricanes. Since 1982, however, Miami has been restoring historic buildings, developing new attractions, and pouring money into the Port of Miami and the rapid-transit system.

The narrow strip of land between the Intracoastal Waterway and the Atlantic Ocean is **Miami Beach.** Here art deco structures and gleaming hotels stretch as far as the eye can see.

THE BEACHES

Southeast Florida has some of the most famous stretches of sand in the world. Beaches are practically everywhere you look, but there are a few special ones you may want to explore. **Fort Lauderdale** beaches are popular with sunseekers of all ages. At **Hollywood Beach,** there's a 2½-mile boardwalk edged with all kinds of shops and restaurants. **Dania Beach** is one of the most attractive beaches and you can even get a permit for a fun clambake on the sand.

Key Biscayne's **Crandon Park Beach** has 4 miles of warm sand lined with palms and sea grapes, so you can always find a shady spot. And **Bill Baggs Cape Florida State Park** at the tip of the island has lots of shallow water and a historic lighthouse to tour. No matter where you go, you're bound to find a stretch of sand just right for you.

What's That?

HENRY MORRISON FLAGLER MUSEUM

If you're interested in history, the Henry Morrison Flagler Museum is a neat place to see. Flagler's home, Whitehall, was built in 1901 by this Standard Oil millionaire who developed the East Coast of Florida from Jacksonville to Key West with the building of his railroad. Today his home is an impressive museum dedicated to preserving Florida's history. Flagler's private railroad car, named Rambler, was built in 1886. It has been restored and is also on exhibit.

SOUTH FLORIDA SCIENCE MUSEUM AND PLANETARIUM

Don't pass up a chance to see South Florida Science Museum and Planetarium. Chemistry, physics, biology, space science, adaptive anatomy, and marine science are all explored through hands-on exhibits. The Gibson Observatory has viewings of the heavens one night a week, weather permitting. A visit to this special museum makes learning fun.

LOXAHATCHEE NATIONAL WILDLIFE REFUGE

While you're in this area, be sure to stop at Loxahatchee National Wildlife Refuge at the Palm Beach entrance to the Everglades. It's a 221-square-mile national wildlife refuge with recreation areas on each end. Take an exciting airboat ride, fish for bass, and see alligators up close. (Though not *too* close!) If you look carefully, you're bound to see some interesting birds, too.

LITTLE HAVANA

For a taste of Cuba head to Little Havana, the famous Latin quarter of Miami, between downtown Miami and Coral Gables. Little Havana gets its name from the mostly Cuban background of the people who live here.

Calle Ocho (pronounced *Ca-ye O-cho*) is the main street in Little Havana. It's lined with sidewalk cafes, colorful boutiques, and factories where workers still roll cigars by hand. You'll find that fun-loving people greet you with heavy Spanish accents. Brush up on your Spanish and make new friends who will be impressed with your attempts to speak *their* language.

VIZCAYA

Did you ever imagine you'd have a chance to wander through a Renaissance palace? Well, you can. Vizcaya may look out of place in Miami, but that's what makes it so much fun.

Did you know?

Calle Ocho means "8th Street."

Did you know?

Over 1,000 craftsmen worked on Vizcaya for more than 2 years!

■ ■ ■

Since 1952, Dade County Art Museum has operated within the walls of this palace.

International Harvester heir James Deering had this 70-room Italian Renaissance–style palace built in 1916 to house his priceless collection of European and Oriental art. Pretend you're royalty as you investigate its many rooms, formal gardens, and 20 acres of untouched jungle overlooking Biscayne Bay.

MIAMI MUSEUM OF SCIENCE AND SPACE TRANSIT PLANETARIUM

How would you like to tickle a tarantula? Bounce a laser beam? Whisper across a crowded room? You can do all this and more at the Miami Museum of Science and Space Transit Planetarium across the street from Vizcaya. There are over 140 hands-on exhibits where you can make giant soap bubbles or watch your hair stand on end.

In the 65-foot dome planetarium you can journey through a mysterious Black Hole in the heavens. Laser-beam light shows are popular attractions, too.

PLANET OCEAN

Do you know why the ocean has high tides and low tides? At Planet Ocean, more than 100 exhibits tell a fascinating story of the ocean. Find out why the sea is important in our lives. Witness the birth of the oceans. Touch Florida's only iceberg. Climb inside a submarine. There's lots to learn here.

MGM'S *Bounty*
■■■■■■■■■■■■■■

Walk the decks of MGM's *Bounty*, a replica of the full-rigged ship made famous by Fletcher Christian's mutiny against Captain Bligh. The *Bounty* was built by MGM in 1960 and has sailed over 70,000 miles—including her maiden voyage to Tahiti for the filming of *Mutiny on the Bounty*, starring Marlon Brando and Trevor Howard.

MIAMI'S ART DECO DISTRICT
■■■■■■■■■■■■■■■■■■■■■■■■■■■■

One of the most interesting things to see in Miami Beach is the Art Deco District, nearly 80 blocks and 800 buildings surrounding Flamingo Park. These bold geometric patterns and dazzling colors were popular in the 1920s and 1930s. The Miami Design Preservation League offers interesting walking tours of the area.

CORAL GABLES
■■■■■■■■■■■■■■■■

Just south of Miami's Little Havana is the unique suburb of Coral Gables. The city gets its name from the hard coral rock that lies just a few inches below the soil. You'll enjoy exploring this area. Take one of the city's bus tours, or drop by the Coral Gables Chamber of Commerce for a map of the area listing over 100 sights.

If your time is limited, there are a few musts to see. Head first to the **Venetian Municipal Pool,** often

Did you know?

Coral Gables was one of the first completely planned communities in the United States.

called the "World's Most Beautiful Swimmin' Hole." Hewn from solid coral rock, it attracts visitors from all over the world.

Next, stop at **Coral Gables House,** the boyhood home of city developer George Edgar Merrick. It was built in 1898 of locally quarried coral rock.

CORAL CASTLE

Did you know?

Leedskalnin built Coral Castle for a woman he loved whom the townspeople never saw. She left him the night before they were to be married.

Are you ready for a mystery? In a small town south of Miami called Homestead, you'll find Coral Castle. A 97-pound Latvian immigrant named Edward Leedskalnin built the castle entirely by himself between 1925 and 1940. No one knows how he did it! Leedskalnin cut and put into place huge pieces of coral rock—and he did it without any modern machinery. When curious neighbors came to spy, he would sense their presence and quit working until they left. Coral Castle remains a mystery to this day.

Are There Any Animals?

LION COUNTRY SAFARI

If you've always wanted to go on an African safari, here's your chance. Lion Country Safari, 15 miles west of West Palm Beach, is an exciting adventure through a 640-acre wildlife preserve. You can see over 1,000 species of animals roaming free. Make sure you leave your car windows rolled up. They will be the only things between you and the animals! Your safari may be interrupted by tons of rhinos or a herd of elephants lumbering across the road. Remember, they have the right-of-way. Are *you* going to argue with a rhinoceros? You can drive through the park as many times as you like, and each time you'll see something different. Don't forget your camera for this trip. Your friends back home will think you're a photographer for *National Geographic*.

Make sure you stop in at Safari World, where you can see more animals, play games, and thrill to amusement park rides. Visit the petting zoo, or take a junior jungle safari and see llamas, wallabies, and giant tortoises. And if you get hungry, there are plenty of snack bars and restaurants throughout the park.

DREHER PARK ZOO

The Dreher Park Zoo is a more traditional way of observing animals. Here you can see more than 100 species of animals. Some are rare and endangered. Wander through a colorful butterfly exhibit or cuddle a lamb in the petting zoo. There are special weekend programs and Sunday afternoon concerts.

OCEAN WORLD

Would you like to hand-feed a shark? Touch an alligator? Pet a dolphin? Be kissed by a sea lion? You can do all this and more at Fort Lauderdale's Ocean World, a fun place to spend the day. Don't miss the special training demonstrations and sight-seeing boat tours.

MIAMI METROZOO

More than 100 species of animals from all over the world roam cageless on 225 miles of jungles, plains, and forests—separated from you by moats and other natural barriers—at the Miami Metrozoo. Be sure to pick up a map and schedule when you arrive so that you can plan your day around the various show times.

The animals have escaped! Help the zookeeper round them up in alphabetical order so that he can be sure he's caught them all.

_____ panther
_____ elephant
_____ hippopotamus
_____ wallaby
_____ llama
_____ giraffe
_____ tortoise
_____ lion
_____ anteater
_____ jaguar
_____ zebra
_____ monkey
_____ rhinoceros
_____ tiger
_____ black bear
_____ armadillo
_____ Key deer
_____ panda
_____ alligator
_____ orangutan

(Answers on page 146)

Watch a rare white Bengal tiger strolling in front of a replica of an ancient Cambodian temple or spy on an Indian rhinoceros and Himalayan black bear in the Asian Forest Plain. You can even play with gentle animals in the petting zoo, or ride an elephant. If you straddle one of these lumbering pachyderms, make sure you get a photograph to show your friends back home.

MIAMI SEAQUARIUM

Just 3 miles south of Miami on Rickenbacker Causeway is an exciting "zoo" for marine animals. The Miami Seaquarium is the home of Flipper, the performing dolphin who had his own television show in the 1960s. Flipper still entertains visitors at the original Seaquarium TV and movie set where he plays football and soccer with his dolphin pals, Hollywood and Dawn, and rescues his trainer from a burning boat.

A monorail train gives aerial tours of the 60-acre park and facility for important marine research. You can visit most of the exhibits on foot, however. You'll see sharks, exotic fish, endangered Florida manatees, and dozens of aquariums filled with colorful tropical fish.

PARROT JUNGLE

For a change of pace, head for Parrot Jungle, home of the world's most colorful and unusual collection of tropical birds. Trained parrots and macaws jump rope, rollerskate, and even ride bicycles on high wires. Many varieties of birds fly freely in this natural subtropical jungle . . . and some will even eat right out of your hand.

MONKEY JUNGLE

At Monkey Jungle, *you're* the one on exhibit. In this 20-acre jungle, the monkeys roam freely while you watch from inside people cages. These are enclosed walkways that run through the park. Wander through the jungles of Asia, South America, Europe, and Africa—including a 5-acre Amazonian rain forest. The monkeys are a riot. They're silly, serious, loud, and very curious. Do you see some of your little brother or sister's personality in them?

T·R·A·V·E·L D·I·A·R·Y

My favorite animal is the _____, because _____. It looks like _____. Some of the most unusual animals I saw were _____. If I could take an animal home from Florida with me, I'd choose a _____, because _____. I'd name it _____.

❖ ❖ ❖

Are We Having Fun Yet?

SIX FLAGS ATLANTIS

For a day of splashing good fun, take a drive over to Six Flags Atlantis, the world's largest water theme park. Sixty-five acres of wave pools, water slides, chutes, and rides will keep you cool in the warm Florida sun.

A Kiddiecove provides hours of fun for the younger kids. And a visit to Bugs Bunny™ in Looney Tunes™ Land, a playground especially for kids, is always a lot of fun.

Don't miss the Splashmania High Dive and Ski Show featuring daredevil stunts. Concerts are given frequently by popular performers. And when you want to get back into the action, head for the bumper boats or the Triple Drop, an exciting water slide. For some quieter fun, grab an inner tube and float down the Lazy River.

T·H·E F·L·O·R·I·D·A K·E·Y·S

The Keys are unlike any other part of Florida. There's a small-town, laid-back feeling here—time seems to stand still. Where else can you get up early in the morning to watch the sun rise over the Atlantic Ocean and then, at night, walk to the other side of your island to watch the sun set into the Gulf of Mexico?

The Florida Keys stretch for 180 miles over 42 bridges, from Miami to just 90 miles off of Havana, Cuba. Only one highway connects 32 of the islands. It's called the Overseas Highway (U.S. 1).

The people of the Keys have an unusual way of giving their addresses. They don't use house numbers and street names—that's too ordinary. Instead, they give you directions by using mile markers—the small green signs with white numbers you see all along the right shoulder of the Overseas Highway.

THE FLORIDA KEYS

Gulf of Mexico

N

FLORIDA BAY

KEY LARGO

Plantation Key

Windley Key

Upper Matecumbe Key

ISLAMORADA

Lower Matecumbe Key

Grassy Key

Long Key

Big Pine Key

Sugarloaf Key

MARATHON

KEY WEST

ATLANTIC OCEAN

Did you know?

The mile markers—also called mileposts—end with the zero marker in Key West.

What's That?

KEY LARGO

The first Key, and the largest of all the islands, is Key Largo, where you'll find **John Pennekamp Coral Reef Park,** the first underwater park in the United States. This 78-square-mile living reef harbors 40 types of coral and at least 300 species of fish and sea creatures. You can take a trip out to the reef in a glass-bottom boat, where you'll get a spectacular view of colorful tropical fish, sea urchins, curious barracudas, and unusual reef formations up close. If you're more adventurous, rent some snorkeling gear for a fascinating underwater treat. No previous experience is necessary—trained divers are there to help you. If you're a certified scuba diver there's even more of this park for you to explore.

Although this is the most spectacular sight in Key Largo, there's lots more to do. There are nature trails, beaches, windsurfer and Hobie Cat rentals, and even an undersea art gallery. You can also explore *The African Queen*, the actual boat used in the 1951 film with Humphrey Bogart and Katharine Hepburn.

Help Gulliver spot the fish hiding in the coral. How many are there?

(Answers on page 146)

ISLAMORADA

Islamorada—the "Purple Isles"—is the centerpiece of a group of islands that include Plantation Key, Windley Key, Upper Matecumbe Key, Lower Matecumbe Key, and Long Key.

Here you'll find extraordinary sportfishing and game fishing. In fact, the town considers itself the world's sportfishing capital. If you'd rather get in the water, there are plenty of areas to explore with either snorkel or scuba gear, and one of the loveliest natural beaches in all the Keys.

Theater of the Sea on Windley Key is a treat for the entire family. Trained dolphins, sea lions, and turtles put on an exciting show—you may even get to join in!

Did you know?

Islamorada was named for the color early Spanish explorers saw from their ships. The purple color was created by purple snail shells covering the beach.

Did you know?

Theater of the Sea, established in 1946, is the world's 2nd-oldest marine park.

MARATHON

Marathon claims to have the world's longest fishing pier. The pier is made up of 12 miles of former bridges closed to automobiles since the Overseas Highway renovation in 1982.

The spectacular **Seven-Mile Bridge,** one of the nation's first great engineering marvels, starts at Knight's Key. The bridge, originally built by Henry Morrison Flagler for his Overseas Railroad, is actually 110 feet short of 7 miles.

Did you know?

Rangers say the best time to see Key deer is early morning or late afternoon. But if you're patient, you can usually spot one at any time of the day.

■ ■ ■

In 1929, a 30-foot, $10,000 bat tower was built on Sugarloaf Key to attract bats to rid the island of mosquitoes. It didn't work, but you can still see the tower.

THE LOWER KEYS

The Lower Keys abound with unspoiled tropical wilderness. Perhaps the best-known sight here is the **National Key Deer Wildlife Refuge** on Big Pine Key. These small deer are so friendly they'll come right up to you looking for handouts. But please don't feed the Key deer or any wildlife. Hand-fed wild animals can lose their fear of humans, making them more vulnerable to harm.

As you drive down the road, you may notice nests perched on power poles lining the road. They belong to giant ospreys or "sea hawks."

Looe Key National Marine Sanctuary and **Great White Heron National Wildlife Refuge** are also wonderful protected areas to explore. Make sure you have your camera in hand for any surprises.

KEY WEST

Key West, at the very end of the Overseas Highway, is the destination of most tourists who come to the Florida Keys. It's a small island, only 5 miles long and 3½ miles wide, and it has a wonderfully friendly atmosphere.

If this is your first time to Key West, hop aboard the **Conch Tour Train** or the **Old Town Trolley** for one of the most interesting narrated guided tours you'll ever take. Your guide will point out the fascinating sights and provide amusing anecdotes. If you want to tour the town on your own, rent a bicycle or moped or put on your walking shoes. Most attractions are within easy walking distance.

Ernest Hemingway lived in Key West for 30 years— from 1931 to 1961. You can visit his home, where he wrote *For Whom the Bell Tolls*, *A Farewell to Arms*, and *Snows of Kilimanjaro*. **Hemingway Home and Museum,** built in 1851, has remained just as the

Did you know?

Key West was originally called *Cayo Hueso* ("the Island of Bones") by the Spanish.

■ ■ ■

The main trade of Key West was once "wrecking." So many ships were wrecked on these coral shores that everyone on the island was involved in salvaging treasures from these vessels.

author left it, and sons and daughters of his 6-toed cats roam the grounds at will.

Guides will lead you from room to room, pointing out interesting architectural features and personal belongings. A swimming pool in the courtyard—the first built in this city—has a penny stuck in the cement. Hemingway put it there, claiming it took his last penny to build the pool.

You can also visit **Audubon House,** a restored mansion where John James Audubon stayed while painting the wildlife of the Florida Keys. Here you'll see period furnishings and antiques, as well as one of Audubon's few intact "Double Elephant Folios." Captain John Geiger, the owner of this house, was a sea captain and master wrecker. He hauled many of the house's furnishings off sinking ships.

T·R·A·V·E·L D·I·A·R·Y

The Florida Keys are fun to visit. I saw _____. My favorite place was _____. That's because _____ _____

❖ ❖ ❖

Other famous people have spent time in Key West. Tennessee Williams, Pulitzer prize–winning playwright, lived here for 34 years until his death in 1983. Today Key West is best known as the home of balladeer Jimmy Buffet and his Coral Reefer Band.

Wander out to the **Lighthouse Military Museum.** You can climb to the top of the historic light, look through a submarine periscope, and explore nearly ½ acre of military hardware. The most unusual thing you'll see here is a midget submarine that was launched by the Japanese navy during World War II. It's one of only 2 still in existence!

Did you know?

Tennessee Williams wrote *The Glass Menagerie, A Streetcar Named Desire,* and *Cat on a Hot Tin Roof.*

The **Wrecker's Museum,** Key West's oldest house and home of Captain Francis B. Watlinton, gives you an interesting look at the "rules" of wrecking. It's funny to think that there were actually rules governing what was really stealing.

Key West Hunt

Gulliver is organizing a scavenger hunt. Draw a line from the items on his list to the places where they can most likely be found.

penny stuck in cement	Audubon House
wildlife paintings	Mel Fisher's Treasure Exhibit
submarine periscope	Mallory Pier
early cigar labels	Hemingway Home and Museum
gold doubloon	Lighthouse Military Museum
mimes & jugglers	East Martello Art Gallery and Museum

(Answers on page 147)

Did you know?

The earliest industries in this island town were wrecking, sponging, salt manufacturing, cigar making, turtle canning, and rum running.

Climb the 48-step winding staircase to the top of the citadel for a fantastic view of the land and ocean. This massive fort was built to protect the nation's southernmost border prior to the American Civil War. Today it's the **East Martello Art Gallery and Museum,** where there are displays of the early cigar-making, sponging, and railroad industries. One of the most fascinating exhibits brings the world of pirates and wrecking to life. Local artists display their paintings here, too.

If it's treasure you fancy, don't miss **Mel Fisher's Treasure Exhibit.** Mel Fisher is the world's best-known treasure seeker. The gold and silver, precious stones, jewelry, coins, and artifacts he has recovered from sunken galleons are on display here. The most famous Spanish galleons he has discovered on the ocean floor are *Nuestro Señora de Atocha* and the *Santa Margarita,* both of which sank in 1622.

Did you know?

When you hold a conch shell to your ear to hear sea sounds, what you're really hearing is air going through the shell.

Shortly before sunset, people begin to gather at **Mallory Pier.** Jugglers, fire-eaters, acrobats, para-sailors, bongo-drum players, and pirates fill the evening air with a carnival-like atmosphere. Peddlers hawk their wares and musicians play. What's this all about? Nature, of course. Tourists and Key West residents join together every evening to witness the most spectacular Key West attraction of all—the Sunset Celebration. As the huge, glowing sun drops off the edge of the universe, you hear "oohs and aahs," followed by applause. For a brief moment, time stands still. Then the entertainers stow their gear and the visitors drift off, knowing that the next day they will meet again to celebrate the sunset.

Are There Any Animals?

DOLPHINS

If you've ever thought about swimming with a dolphin, here's your chance! There are 4 places where you can swim freely with these gentle, intelligent creatures. It's expensive for a brief encounter, but where else could you find such an opportunity?

At Key Largo's **Dolphin's Plus,** visitors and residents are welcomed for swim sessions. The operation is concentrating its efforts on handicapped children, but it welcomes other visitors as well.

Theater of the Sea, the marine park in Islamorada, also offers dolphin rides 3 times a day. And on the grounds of Hawk's Cay Resort, near Marathon, you'll find **Zoovet Productions,** a training facility for dolphins on their way to animal shows for major U.S. attractions. But you have to be a guest of Hawk's Cay to go for a swim here.

The **Dolphin Research Center** on Grassy Key is a nonprofit teaching and research facility. Here they believe that the dolphins enjoy contact with people and that the "swimmers" are a form of fun and entertainment for the dolphins, rather than the other way around. It's an interesting way of looking at things.

KEY WEST AQUARIUM

Key West Aquarium, in operation since 1932, was the first tourist attraction built in the Keys and the first open-air aquarium built in the United States. Its living coral reef offers a great view of the sea life that makes its home in the struggling coral system. Barracuda, hammerhead shark, and parrot fish swim in this undersea world. Shark tanks and a turtle pool are also of interest here.

TURTLE KRAALS

The Turtle Kraals play host to a number of turtles, sharks, rays, octopuses, and tropical fish. There's also a turtle cannery museum and a restaurant—no, they don't serve turtles! Turtles are on the endangered species list and are protected from hunters.

THE EVERGLADES

Journey into the mysterious seas of saw grass stretching for miles and miles. Here, amid slow-moving shallow waters, you'll discover some of nature's most fascinating gifts.

The Everglades is made up of a variety of ecosystems, each depending upon the others for survival. And the plant and animal life found in each is quite different.

The Everglades teem with animal life. Black bears, panthers, white-tailed deer, mink, otters, and manatee are among the many mammals that live in this region. More than 300 different species of birds also live here. And giant loggerhead turtles grow to 300 pounds, while the alligator thrives in this wet, wild region.

Did you know?

An ecosystem is a community and its environment working together as an ecological unit in nature.

・・・

The Eastern diamondback rattlesnake lives in the pinelands of the Everglades. It can reach up to 8 feet in length and its bite is among the deadliest of all the world's venomous snakes.

THE EVERGLADES

FORT MYERS

CORKSCREW SWAMP SANCTUARY

EVERGLADES WONDER GARDENS

BIG CYPRESS NATIONAL PRESERVE

NAPLES

Gulf of Mexico

Shark Valley

MIAMI

Miccosukee Indian Village

EVERGLADES NATIONAL PARK

Visitor Center

Flamingo

Florida Bay

ATLANTIC OCEAN

What's That?

EVERGLADES NATIONAL PARK

Everglades National Park was established in 1947 as a means of protecting 1.4 million acres of fragile ecosystems. In all the world there's nothing quite like Florida's Everglades. But some experts think it's only a matter of time before man destroys this fragile environment where nature's interdependence is so important.

At the **Main Visitor Center,** west of Homestead, you'll receive a crash course in identifying important features of the Everglades. Knowing what things to look for is half the fun; seeing them is the other half.

The Everglades also play host to countless pests of the biting kind, such as mosquitoes and deerflies. They love to feast on unprepared visitors, so bring plenty of good insect repellent (or buy it at the Visitors Center) . . . the stronger the better. Don't offer yourself for lunch!

Make sure you pick up a map and brochure at the Visitors Center—and don't miss viewing the short film, which will help to make your trip more

Did you know?

Everglades National Park is larger than the state of Delaware.

＿ ＿ ＿

Water flows through the Everglades at a rate of about 1/2 mile per day.

＿ ＿ ＿

There are 45 indigenous species of plants here that can be found nowhere else in the world.

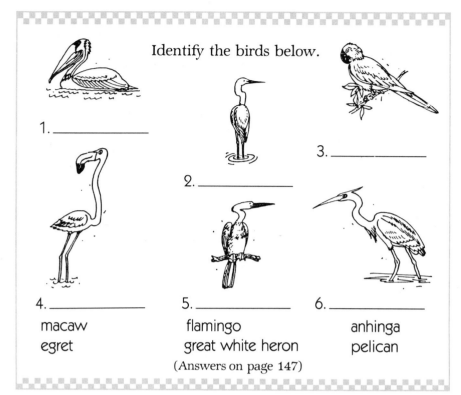

Identify the birds below.

1. _____

2. _____

3. _____

4. _____

5. _____

6. _____

macaw
egret

flamingo
great white heron

anhinga
pelican

(Answers on page 147)

(Answers on page 147)

(Answers on page 147)

meaningful. Then, as you travel along Ingraham Highway—the only road into and out of Everglades National Park—plan stops along the way or you'll miss the most important sights. You'll find trails, observation decks, and visitor centers along the 38-mile road to Flamingo. But remember, some parts of the Everglades are still uncharted, so stick to the boardwalks and marked trails. And *don't* try to pet an alligator!

One of the many interesting sights to see can be found on the **Mahogany Hammock Trail,** which takes you under some of the largest mahogany trees in the United States. If you prefer a canoe to a car, paddle down the **Noble Hammock Canoe Trail,** a 2½-mile loop through mangrove clusters.

Did you know?

There are about 100 species of grass in the Everglades.

■ ■ ■

Saw grass is not really grass, but a sedge.

Did you know?

At Canepatch, you'll see wild sugarcane, limes, bananas, and papaya growing. Calusa and Seminole Indians raised these crops here until 1928, when their settlement disappeared.

88

Did you know?

Alligators make a variety of sounds. Beware: A hiss usually means that they are annoyed and you'd better stay out of their way! Never argue with an alligator!

Speak and Spell

Here are some more places that have been given Indian names.

Name	Indian Meaning
Palatka	ferry crossing
Hialeah	prairie
Homosassa	place of peppers
Tampa	stick of fire

At **Flamingo**, Ingraham Highway loops around and heads back the way you came. But this isn't the end of your adventure, for there are campsites for motor homes and tents and a motel. If you plan to explore on your own, either by boat or hiking trail, be sure to notify the ranger station before setting out. Even skilled sportsmen have been known to disappear into the Everglades, never to return.

If you pass the main entrance to Everglades National Park, there's another way to explore this area. The **Shark Valley** entrance is mostly underwater in the summer, but in the winter there's an exciting tram ride to an observation tower. Ask a ranger to imitate the bellow of an alligator and you'll see dozens of these reptiles glide out from the brush.

MICCOSUKEE INDIAN VILLAGE AND CULTURE CENTER

Across the street from the Shark Valley entrance to Everglades National Park is the Miccosukee Indian Village. Take a guided tour and experience Indian life. Here tribal members still create and exhibit their crafts. There's even an Indian Museum that features films and artifacts from different Indian tribes. If you tire of this, you can always take a wild, bumpy airboat ride through the Everglades.

BIG CYPRESS NATIONAL PRESERVE

You'll be fascinated by the stillness of Big Cypress National Preserve, home to unusual and mysterious creatures for thousands of years. Much of it has still not been explored completely by humans. Big Cypress Swamp was the last refuge of the Seminoles after their leader, Osceola, was imprisoned by land-hungry white men many years ago. Take time to hike the trails and explore the unusual plant life. And keep your eyes open for paw prints of the rare Florida panthers or black bears that live in these parts.

CORKSCREW SWAMP SANCTUARY

You can view more mysteries of the Everglades at an 11,000-acre wildlife park near Naples. At Corkscrew Swamp Sanctuary you'll see beautiful orchids, huge ferns, and unusual birds. But keep your eyes open. What you think is a log might be an alligator.

Did you know?

Big Cypress Swamp covers 2,400 square miles.

EVERGLADES WONDER GARDENS

Did you know?

A wood stork stands about 3½ feet tall and has a wingspan of nearly 6 feet. At Corkscrew Swamp, you can see more than 1,000 nests high overhead.

You may think you've traveled to a distant planet when you visit Lester Piper's Everglades Wonder Gardens. You'll see endangered species such as the Florida panther, black bear, American crocodiles, and alligators. Guides will alert you to the various types of poisonous snakes that live in this region. Whatever you do, don't forget your camera.

T·H·E W·E·S·T
C·O·A·S·T

The Gulf water temperature ranges from 64° in January to a warm 86° in August and September.

■ ■ ■

West Coast beaches have the whitest and finest sand found anywhere in the world.

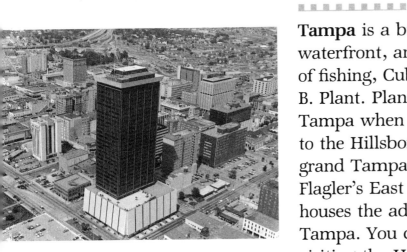

Florida's West Coast is frequently called the Gulf Coast because of its location on the Gulf of Mexico. This is the Florida you see in travel advertisements— fine, snow-white beaches; calm, crystal-clear waters; swaying palm trees; and the ever-present warmth of the sun. It's the perfect place to relax. But there's a wealth of amusement waiting for the adventurous visitor.

THE CITIES

Tampa is a big city with small-town charm, a fine waterfront, and many things to do. Its history speaks of fishing, Cuban cigars, pirates, and the great Henry B. Plant. Plant was a railroad tycoon who developed Tampa when he extended his South Florida Railroad to the Hillsborough River in 1884. He then built the grand Tampa Bay Hotel to rival Henry Morrison Flagler's East Coast hotel empire. Today the old hotel houses the administrative offices of the University of Tampa. You can catch a glimpse of Tampa's past by visiting the Henry B. Plant Museum, just off the lobby.

91

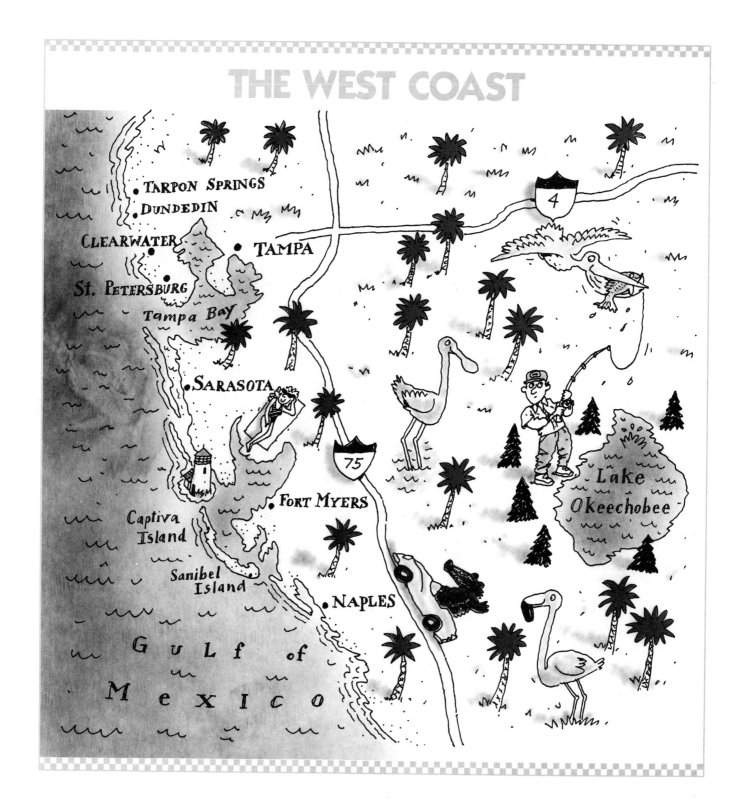

The 8 resort communities between St. Petersburg and Tarpon Springs make up what is commonly known as Florida's Pinellas Suncoast—28 miles of white sand beaches fringed by the warm, sapphire waters of the Gulf of Mexico.

St. Petersburg, on the southernmost end of the Pinellas peninsula, is bordered on 3 sides by water and has earned the title of "Sailing Capital of the South." It's one of the prettiest waterfront cities in Florida. *The Guinness Book of World Records* lists St. Petersburg as having the longest stretch of sunshine—768 consecutive days, from February 9, 1967, to March 17, 1969. That's a lot of sun!

St. Petersburg Beach, Treasure Island, Madeira Beach, Indian Rocks Beach, Clearwater, Clearwater Beach, Dunedin, and Tarpon Springs make up the remaining 7 towns of the Pinellas Suncoast. Each has its own special attractions and beauty.

Whatever you do, don't miss the sunset here on the West Coast. It's breathtaking.

White sand beaches, art galleries and theaters, charming streets—that's **Sarasota,** best known as the city of circus king John Ringling. Ringling built his home here in the 1920s for an estimated $2 million and encouraged his wealthy friends to do likewise. Today it's a very special city with wonderful attractions ranging from the glistening beaches to John Ringling's awesome estate.

The **Fort Myers** area is everything you think of when Florida is mentioned—towering palm trees, white beaches, warm sunshine, and clear blue water. Included in this area is the island paradise of Sanibel and Captiva, two small islands just off the coast of Fort Myers. You'll relax while you swim, snorkel, build sand castles, boat, fish, and, most important in these parts, collect shells.

THE BEACHES

The West Coast is known the world over for its white beaches and powdery sand. And the calm, blue waters of the Gulf of Mexico are perfect for swimming. No need to worry about getting pounded by waves here—they're over on the Atlantic Coast. The water is warm and the days are sunny. What more could you ask for?

The Gulf Coast beaches are considered Florida's finest and it's easy to see why. A few have certain distinctions over the others. **Fort Myers Beach** on Estero Island is known as "the World's Safest Beach." Its sandy bottom slopes gradually into the Gulf, so you avoid any surprises of suddenly being in water over your head. The beach is wide and the white sand is soft. And beachcombing on **Venice** beaches will yield a bounty of fossilized sharks' teeth. But the most famous of all the Gulf Coast beaches are on Sanibel and Captiva islands.

Sanibel Island and **Captiva Island** beaches are world famous for their glistening white sand and abundance of seashells. In fact, Sanibel Island is considered one of the best shelling beaches in the world—number 3, to be exact. Once you get a taste of the pleasure of shelling, you'll be hooked. Over 400 species of shells wash up on the sands, from the common clam and scallop to the rare tulips, olives, and the rarest of them all, the brown-speckled junonia. Head over to any one of the many gift shops and pick up an inexpensive shelling guide so that you know what you're finding. Then head for the beach.

Did you know?

Sanibel Island's boomerang shape and east-west direction encourages shelling because it slows down the shells and brings them onto the beach in one piece.

You'll want to be able to identify the shells you find on the beaches of Florida. Place the name of the shell below its picture.

1. _____

2. _____

3. _____

4. _____

5. _____

6. _____

Which of these shells are univalves? _____
Which are bivalves? _____

junonia   scallop
tulip   olive
common clam   conch

(Answers on page 147)

The easiest way to shell is called beachcombing. That means you search along the tide line for dead shells that have been washed up by the gentle waves. You can put together a fine collection in a single day. Or you can visit one of the shell shops and purchase what you're missing. No one else will ever know you didn't find it yourself.

Did you know?

The taking of live shells is restricted to 2 live shells per species per person. (In the J. N. Ding Darling National Wildlife Refuge, no live shells may be taken.)

■ ■ ■

If a bivalve (a shell with 2 hinged sections, like a clam) is tightly closed, or an operculum (a shell with a trapdoor) is shut, or if an animal withdraws into its shell when touched, you have a live shell. Help these creatures by placing them back in the water and burying them in the sand (not too deep) once they've withdrawn into their shells.

Did you know?

Although Sanibel Island is the prime shelling beach in the United States, other area beaches are not to be overlooked. They have tons of beautiful shells on their shores as well.

It's best to get to the beach early in the morning, before the shells have been picked over. Some addicted beachcombers go out at night wearing miners' head lamps or carrying flashlights to beat the early morning crowd. That's dedication!

At the end of a long day of shelling, you'll be surprised to discover that you, too, have a severe case of "Sanibel stoop," the bent-over position that's a familiar sight along the beaches from sunrise to sunset.

What's That?

YBOR CITY

Tampa's Latin Quarter, Ybor City (pronouced *EE-bor*), is a lively, colorful tribute to the Cuban, Italian, and Spanish immigrants whose lives centered around a flourishing cigar industry that began over 100 years ago.

The former V. M. Ybor Cigar Factory has become home to one of Tampa's most interesting shopping arcades, **Ybor Square, Ltd.** Here you'll find specialty shops, restaurants, arts and crafts stores, and even a place where cigars are still rolled by hand.

Did you know?

Ybor City was named for Vincente Martinez Ybor, who came from Cuba to Tampa in 1885 to manufacture cigars.

■ ■ ■

Three million cigars a day are still produced here.

■ ■ ■

Automation eventually put most of the cigar factories out of business.

Did you know?

Hundreds of workers would sit at long benches tediously shaping prized cigars while a "reader" sat on a platform entertaining them with selections from poetry, books, and newspapers.

For an in-depth look at the cigar industry and the city's past, go to the **Ybor City State Museum.** Built in the renovated Ferlita Bakery, the museum contains an interesting collection of cigar labels depicting the city's culture. Near the museum is **Ybor City Preservation Park,** where 6 restored original cigar workers' houses give you a glimpse of what home life was like for these workers.

MUSEUM OF SCIENCE AND INDUSTRY

Experience a 75-mph hurricane, a Florida thunderstorm, or incredible optical illusions at Tampa's Museum of Science and Industry. Here you can explore the mysteries of science through hands-on exhibits.

You'll learn about the sun, weather, electricity, geology, plants, and fiber optics—and have fun at the same time. There are tons of things to play with! And there's even a Discovery Room where preschoolers can investigate the world of science, too.

CHILDREN'S MUSEUM OF TAMPA

Grab a cart and go grocery shopping, run a miniature post office, or make giant bubbles. No one will say "Don't touch!" at the Children's Museum of Tampa. Here you'll get to play with all sorts of fun things. You can dress up in costumes, spend a day "at the office," or even make beautiful music. This is your chance to do all the things that you see grown-ups do.

SUNKEN GARDENS

It was once a sinkhole, but today it's a beautifully land-scaped, botanical paradise. What is it? Why, Sunken Gardens, of course! Seventy years ago George Turner turned this waterlogged sinkhole into a blooming wonderland. More than 50,000 tropical plants and flowers grow year-round here, so don't forget your

Did you know?

The brightly colored pipes you see overhead are color coded according to their job:

Red = air-conditioning supply
Purple = air-conditioning return
Green = air-conditioning intake
Yellow = electricity
Blue = fire sprinklers
Orange = fresh water/drainage

■ ■ ■

Hurricanes can reach speeds of up to 200 mph and release as much energy as 8 billion tons of TNT!

■ ■ ■

The Museum of Science and Industry is the largest museum in Florida and the largest science museum in the Southeast.

camera and color film. For an added treat, take a leisurely stroll in the walk-through aviary or in the fragrant Orchid Arbor.

Did you know?

Sunken Gardens claims to have the world's largest gift shop. What do you think?

Beautiful flowers and tropical plants grow at Sunken Gardens. Color the "photograph" below.

LONDON WAX MUSEUM

Visit Cleopatra, Julius Caesar, Lee Harvey Oswald, and Bluebeard at Louis Tussaud's London Wax Museum in St. Petersburg Beach. Over 100 lifelike wax sculptures of the famous and infamous reside in the museum. You'll see composers, sports heroes, gangsters, world leaders, authors, pirates, and entertainers. And they look so real! For a spine-tingling experience, tour the Chamber of Horrors. But remember, it's not for the faint of heart.

SPONGES

Relive the days when Tarpon Springs was the "Sponge Capital of the World" at **Spongeorama Exhibit Center,** located on Tarpon Springs' famous sponge docks. Here you'll see life-size scenes and animated displays of the early Greek sponge divers. You can also board a boat for a demonstration of sponge diving by an old Greek in his traditional diving suit.

The large Greek population has remained in Tarpon Springs, and although synthetic sponges have largely taken the place of nature's sponges, the sponge industry is still alive here. You'll have to keep reminding yourself that you're in Florida as you walk down the streets of this city. Greek foods and handicrafts are sold in shops. And Greek voices are carried on the breeze from the many coffee shops along side streets.

While you're here, don't miss a stop at the **Sponge Exchange,** where sponges were once stored prior to auction. Today the sponges are gone, but in their place are specialty stores and restaurants combined with exhibits heralding the sponge-diving tradition.

Did you know?

John Corcoris, a Greek sponge buyer, discovered the rich sponge beds of the Gulf of Mexico. He encouraged Greek divers to move to Tarpon Springs and the sponge industry boomed. By 1936, 2,000 Greeks had relocated to Tarpon Springs.

Speak and Spell

You can greet the people of Tarpon Springs with

Ya' sou,

which means hello or good-bye in Greek.

Did you know?

When John Ringling died, he left his 68-acre estate, his priceless art collection, and his entire fortune to the state of Florida.

RINGLING MUSEUM COMPLEX

Sarasota's Ringling Museum Complex stands as a tribute to John Ringling—circus giant, art lover, and master promoter.

Tour the magnificent 30-room mansion that was home for John and Mabel Ringling. Built in the 1920s and patterned after the famous Doges' Palace in

Venice, Italy, it was called **C'ad'zan**, which means "House of John." Don't miss a peek into the bathrooms. Ringling had solid-gold fixtures installed!

But there's more to see than this multimillion-dollar, treasure-filled estate. Ringling had to build a museum to house all the art he had collected. The **John and Mabel Ringling Museum of Art** looks like a 15-century Italian villa.

Did you know?

The 18th-century Asolo Theater in the Ringling complex was brought over from Italy and reassembled here.

Did you know?

Some of Ringling's cars are here, too.

A formal garden sits in the middle of the complex, with galleries on 3 sides and a huge bronze copy of Michelangelo's *David* on the 4th side. Here you can see one of the world's most important collections of works by Flemish painter Peter Paul Rubens. Even if you're not excited by works of art, you'll be awestruck by the magnificence of this museum.

Perhaps the most interesting part of the museum complex is the **Museum of the Circus,** an exciting display of circus memorabilia, calliopes, gilded parade wagons, and posters from the Greatest Show on Earth. Nowhere else can you see the history of the circus in such detail.

BELLM'S CARS AND MUSIC OF YESTERDAY

Car buffs, welcome! Bellm's Cars and Music of Yesterday is a wonderland of automobiles and musical items. It sounds like a strange combination, but it works. Browse among some of the classic (and not-so-classic) cars of yesterday. You'll wonder how some of these cars ever made it down the street, and you'll marvel at the sleek beauty of others. If music is more your style, check out the large collection of music boxes, Victrolas, calliopes, jukeboxes, and more. You'll especially love the 200-piece arcade with antique games. It's a far cry from today's computerized Pac-Man!

SOUTH FLORIDA MUSEUM AND BISHOP PLANETARIUM

Southwest Florida's history comes to life at South Florida Museum and Bishop Planetarium. Take a look at the life-styles of primitive Indians and Civil War soldiers in a fascinating diorama of Florida's history from the Stone Age to the space age. Prehistoric Indian relics and a health museum round out this collection. You can view the heavens in the planetarium, where a Cassegrainian reflecting telescope is opened for a free look at faraway stars on the first and third weekends of every month. Laser light shows are presented regularly.

RINGLING BROTHERS AND BARNUM & BAILEY CIRCUS

Twenty miles south of Sarasota lies the town of Venice, the winter quarters of Ringling Brothers and Barnum & Bailey Circus. Each January, before going on tour, the circus tries out its new routines here. Jugglers, mimes, and acrobats flock to Venice to attend the world-famous **Ringling Clown College**, where nearly 5,000 aspiring clowns train for 60 spots per year.

It's time to get ready for the show under the Big Top, but this clown needs some help in painting his face.

102

THE SHELL FACTORY

Neptune's treasures and more await at the Shell Factory in North Fort Myers. Here you'll find the "world's largest collection of rare shells, corals, sponges, and fossils from the 7 seas." There are oodles of things to choose from—shells, jewelry, clothing, gourmet foods, and all sorts of gift items from around the world. If you get tired of shopping, there's a kid's arcade packed with the latest video games, pinball machines, skeeball, and a Wild West shooting gallery. Or for some real action, take a wild and bouncy ride aboard the Bumper Boats or get behind the wheel of the Can-Am Racing Cars that speed around a twisting track. Don't you wish all stores had their own private amusement parks?

FANTASY ISLES

Right next door to the Shell Factory is Fantasy Isles, a storybook wonderland of fun and magic. Here you can say hello to all of your favorite nursery rhyme characters—Mother Goose, Jack and Jill, Little Boy Blue, Humpty Dumpty . . . they're all here. There are exotic birds and magic shows, a petting zoo, a wax museum, and lots of rides, too. And the Little Engine That Could takes you on a special tour along the banks of lakes and past cascading waterfalls.

Can you figure out which nursery rhyme character is being referred to in the following statements?

1. She's afraid of spiders.

_____

2. He found a plum in his Christmas pie.

_____

3. He's sleeping under a haystack.

_____

4. Her flock is missing.

_____

5. The knave got a beating for stealing her tarts.

_____

6. They lost their mittens and couldn't have any pie.

_____

7. He runs through the town with his night-gown on.

_____

8. He kissed the girls and made them cry.

_____

9. He kept his wife in a pumpkin shell.

_____

10. Cockle shells and silver bells grow in her garden.

_____

(Answers on page 147)

Did you know?

Thomas Edison was diabetic, totally deaf, and had only had 3 months of formal schooling, and yet he was issued 1,093 U.S. patents!

EDISON WINTER HOME MUSEUM

There's a house where light bulbs, installed in 1925, burn an average of 12 hours a day and still have not burned out. Where is this amazing sight? At Edison Winter Home Museum in Fort Myers, of course!

At the age of 38, Thomas Alva Edison was told by his doctor that he was seriously ill and that it was absolutely necessary for him to find a healthier climate. At the time, he was searching for a suitable filament material for his incandescent light bulb, and his search led him to Fort Myers, where he found an abundance of bamboo trees growing along the Caloosahatchee River. Killing two birds with one stone, he used the bamboo for his filament and relied on the warm tropical climate to do wonders for his health. It must have helped because he lived to the ripe old age of 84!

Today you can tour the charming 14-acre waterfront estate where Edison and his wife spent 50 winters together. Everything remains just as the Edisons left it.

Did you know?

Edison's home was one of the first prefabricated buildings in America. The house was built in sections in Fairfield, Maine, in 1885. It was then transported to Fort Myers by 4 ships and erected in 1886.

WALTZING WATERS

Liquid fireworks—that's what you'll find at Waltzing Waters, an exciting, unbelievable performance of spectacular fountains, dazzling colored lights, and beautiful music. Brilliantly colored streams of water dance to music amid an array of special effects made possible through the use of lasers and multimedia equipment. If you're here during the day, you'll witness the spectacle in a darkened auditorium, but if you're lucky enough to be here at night, you'll see the performance in nature's theater—the great outdoors! The huge outdoor show hurls 7,000 gallons per minute nearly 100 feet into the air. It's awesome!

NATURE CENTER AND PLANETARIUM OF LEE COUNTY

Take a tour of an Everglades-style swamp as you stroll along the rustic boardwalk at Nature Center and Planetarium of Lee County. This 100-acre center provides you with a close-up look at the flora and fauna of Florida. There's even an aviary for injured birds. If outer space is more your thing, the planetarium features changing shows and laser effects.

FORT MYERS HISTORICAL MUSEUM

Displays and exhibits documenting the history of the area from as far back as 1200 B.C. can be seen at the Fort Myers Historical Museum, housed in the restored Peck Street Depot. The Calusa and Seminole Indian depictions are fascinating, as are the scale models of the Moger Cigar Factory and C. J. Jones Lumber Mill. The Esperanza, a 1930 private rail car, gives you an unusual look at first-class travel. Several days a week you can see films on art, music, and poetry. Check with the museum for schedules of special exhibits and oral history programs.

SANIBEL LIGHTHOUSE

Lighthouses beckon to be explored, and the one on the eastern tip of Sanibel Island is no exception. It was originally built in 1884 to warn cattle ships, sailing from San Carlos Bay to Key West and Cuba, of the small island's presence. Today its flashing light still alerts passing ships at night.

Did you know?

The Peck Street Depot served rail passengers for 67 years—from 1904 to 1971.

106

Are There Any Animals?

LOWRY PARK ZOO

Tampa's Lowry Park Zoo has recently undergone some major changes. No longer is it an outdated zoo of cages and bored inhabitants. The animals have a new $20-million home where they live in environments that re-create their natural habitat.

Natural barriers, such as moats, separate you from the bears, giraffes, and elephants that live here. Explore Primate World, where monkeys swing from trees and artificial vines, or the Asian Domain, with its black bears, Bengal tigers, elephants, and leopards. There's a walk-through aviary and a petting zoo, too. If you're in Tampa, this zoo shouldn't be missed.

Did you know?

Habitat refers to where an animal normally lives in the wild. This includes climate, vegetation, and geographic features.

SUNCOAST SEABIRD SANCTUARY

Have you ever thought about adopting a bird? You can do just that at the Suncoast Seabird Sanctuary in Indian Shores, a nonprofit organization dedicated to the care of injured and crippled birds. This refuge and rehabilitation center is home to as many as 500 birds at a time. If you're a shutterbug, you'll have a

Did you know?

A successful "foster-parent program" was established in which crippled adult birds raise abandoned young.

great time with the close-up shots you can get of brown pelicans, white herons, seagulls, owls, hawks, and many other birds. You may even run into a well-known wildlife artist or researcher. They often spend a great deal of time studying these birds up close.

SARASOTA JUNGLE GARDENS

Jungle plants and flowers thrive at Sarasota Jungle Gardens. But there's more than vegetation here. Beautiful pink flamingos, regal leopards, alligators, monkeys, and brilliantly colored parrots live in this 16-acre jungle of winding nature trails. There are bird and reptile shows, a shell museum, a butterfly collection, a petting zoo, and a Kiddie Jungle just for kids.

Did you know?

Although the anhinga is a bird that dives for fish, it lacks protective oil coating on its feathers, so after each dive it has to climb a nearby bush and hang itself out to dry.

J. N. DING DARLING NATIONAL WILDLIFE REFUGE

There are many ways to explore nature at the J. N. Ding Darling National Wildlife Refuge on the north side of Sanibel Island. You can take a 5-mile scenic drive that winds through the park past red mangroves, cabbage palms, and other varieties of native plants. But for closer inspection, take a walking tour, or ply the waters in a canoe. You'll encounter native wading birds such as ibis, roseate spoonbills, egrets, ospreys, herons, and anhingas, as well as reptiles, mammals, and marine life. If you're lucky, you may even get to see some of the endangered or threatened species that call this refuge home. Lumbering, gentle manatees, bald eagles, and Atlantic loggerhead turtles have been sighted with amazing frequency here—a treat for any wildlife enthusiast.

JUNGLE LARRY'S AFRICAN SAFARI PARK AND CARIBBEAN GARDENS

Tropical lagoons, exotic palm trees, and magnificent jungle creatures await you at Jungle Larry's African Safari Park and Caribbean Gardens in the town of Naples. Grab your camera, lather on some sunscreen, and set off on an exciting adventure through 52 acres of jungle, where you're sure to see the largest collection of jungle cats in Florida, toothy alligators, brilliantly colored birds, and mischievous monkeys. And don't miss a performance of the park's trained animals or a trip to the petting zoo, where you can cuddle and feed some of the smaller animals. For a close-up look at how they train the wild animals, visit the Animal Training Center. It's a full day of excitement.

SAFARI TRAIL

T·R·A·V·E·L D·I·A·R·Y

There certainly is a lot to see on the Gulf Coast. Of all the places I visited, I liked _____ the best because _____. One of the funniest things I saw was _____. That's not all I did here. I also _____

_____

If I owned the world's best theme park, it would have _____,

_____.

and I'd call it _____

Are We Having Fun Yet?

BUSCH GARDENS, THE DARK CONTINENT

One of the most popular Florida theme park attractions can be found in Tampa—Busch Gardens, the Dark Continent. The exotic world of Africa has been carefully re-created on 300 acres surrounding the Busch Brewery. Stroll through African villages, take in an entertaining show, plunge down a water-flume thrill ride, or climb aboard the Trans-Veldt Railroad where you'll see gazelles, zebras, and lions roaming free on the Serengeti Plain. But if you want to get some really spectacular photographs, join one of the special photo safaris that take you into the Serengeti Plain aboard the park's feed truck.

Belly dancers and snake charmers entertain you in exotic Marrakesh, and huge Bengal tigers prowl in the Congo. Visit Nocturnal Mountain in Nairobi, where you can see animals that normally are awake only at night, such as bats and owls. At the Nairobi Field Station is an unusual nursery. Here newborn animals are cared for by human surrogate mothers. Don't

Did you know?

The animals are most active first thing in the morning, so try to get to the Serengeti Plain early in the day.

111

miss a peek in the playroom, where the baby chimps romp and socialize. They're a riot! For a tummy-losing dose of excitement, don't miss the Python roller coaster. It won't let you go until it has spun you through a 360° loop! What a perspective you'll get if you can keep your eyes open and stop screaming long enough to enjoy it. For a cooler thrill, brave the white water of the Congo River Rapids, or plunge down the flume at Stanley Falls. Don't even *think* you'll stay dry, because you won't!

For quieter fun, tour the Busch Brewery, where bottles zoom by on huge conveyer belts. Or put your feet up and feast your eyes and ears on one of the spectacular shows in Morocco, Timbuktu, or Nairobi. There's a full day of fun waiting for you just inside the gates to the Dark Continent.

ADVENTURE ISLAND

A 13-acre water park next to Busch Gardens promises cool, wet fun for the entire family. At Adventure Island, you can slip and slide down a flume at breakneck speed, splash in a waterfall, or surf the "ocean" waves. If you're really brave, climb 5 stories and plunge at speeds of up to 40 mph down a superslippery slide known as the Gulf Scream. And when you get your breath back, head for Paradise Lagoon. Dive in—or, for a really exciting entry, grab onto the Cable Glide that crosses the pool and . . . let go! If you want to get wet and have some fun, Adventure Island is the place to do it.

Did you know?

More than 1,200 animals are born at Busch Gardens each year.

This 300-acre park contains the largest collection of mammals, birds, and reptiles in North America—3,000 in all!

WEEKI WACHEE

Nature has set the stage for an exciting underwater extravaganza at Florida's Weeki Wachee. Where else can you see beautiful mermaids perform underwater ballets and daring dives in crystal-clear water?

But there's more to Weeki Wachee than mermaids. The Birds of Prey Show features hawks, owls, and other birds exhibiting their natural survival skills. For a little comedy, macaws and cockatoos add their own spontaneity to their performances at the Exotic Birds Show. If you like to be a part of the action, take a Wilderness River Cruise with a stop at Pelican Orphanage. Or stroll along the river to the petting zoo where you can hug a goat, feed a deer, or talk to a bird. The animals love the attention . . . and you'll love it, too.

Did you know?

Weeki Wachee Spring is actually the surfacing point of a huge underground river. It has been explored to a depth of 550 feet, but no one has discovered the bottom yet.

Over 168 million gallons of water flow into the spring each day. That's enough to fill over 5,000 swimming pools!

BUCCANEER BAY

Next door to Weeki Wachee is Buccaneer Bay, a 3½-acre water park where you're invited to splash in the spring, shoot down a flume on a cushion of water, and swing from a rope at Blackbeard's Lagoon. It's wet, cool, fun in the sun.

Did you know?

A number of feature films and TV shows have been shot at Weeki Wachee.

THE NORTHWEST/ PANHANDLE

When you think of Florida, images of palm trees, sandy beaches, Mickey Mouse, alligators, and sea life come to mind. But rarely do you ever think of the desolate white beaches, pine forests, and old Southern charm of Florida's Panhandle. This area is frequently overlooked by tourists, yet it offers a great deal.

114

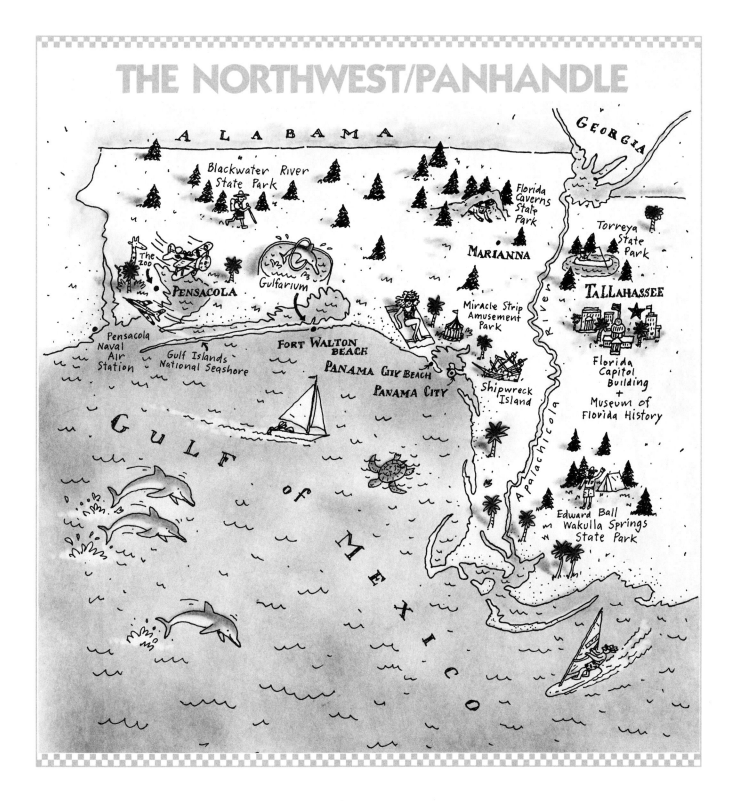

THE NORTHWEST/PANHANDLE

The Northwest area of Florida is known as the Panhandle because it's shaped like the handle of a pan.

• • •

Unlike the rest of Florida, the Panhandle's tourist season is in the spring and summer—from Easter to Labor Day.

The weather is cooler here—averaging 60° in the winter and a breezy 80° in the summer. The sugar-white beaches and smaller crowds are the biggest draws. And there's lots to do—swimming, sunning, sailing, shelling. The Panhandle has its share of attractions, too—historical districts, museums, nature trails, animals, amusement parks, and minature golf. The list could go on and on. But what's most important is that there's a great deal of fun to be had. And that's what you came here for.

THE CITIES

Pensacola is the western gateway to the state of Florida. This coastal city is full of contrasts—charming historical homes, old Spanish forts and battle sites, miles and miles of uncluttered beaches, a bustling downtown, and the largest U.S. naval air station. Much history surrounds this town in the far west corner of the Sunshine State. It's frequently called "the City of Five Flags" because, at varying times since Spanish settlers first landed here in 1559, it has been under the rule of Spain, England, France, the Confederacy, and the United States. It that sounds like a lot to you, there's more. The government changed 17 times as Pensacola was passed back and forth among these countries!

Silky-soft beaches and a lively amusement park help to create what some call "the Coney Island of the South." From May to September, people flock to **Panama City** to soak up the sun and play in the amusement park. Once you see this city, you won't be able to sit still—you'll want to go, go, go . . . on all the rides, that is. It's the perfect place for family vacations. You can visit a wax museum or a reptile park, play miniature golf, and go beachcombing. Panama City will give you days of never-ending, laughing good fun.

Tallahassee, the state capital of this land of sunshine, welcomes you with Southern hospitality. In 1824, Tallahassee was chosen to be the site of the state capital as a compromise between St. Augustine and Pensacola's desire to be the seat of government. Here you'll find an unusual combination of old Southern mansions and modern office buildings. For a really spectacular view of the city, take an elevator ride to the 22nd floor observation deck of the Florida state capitol. On an extraclear day, you can see all the way to the Gulf!

Did you know?

Tallahassee was the only Confederate state capital east of the Mississippi not captured by Federal forces during the American Civil War.

117

THE BEACHES

The Panhandle region is blessed with miles of undeveloped beaches, many of which have not yet been "discovered" by tourists. Make sure you bring your sunglasses when you visit. The whiteness of the sand can be blinding!

There are 150 miles of unspoiled offshore islands and keys stretching from Gulfport, Mississippi, to Destin, Florida. This is known as **Gulf Islands National Seashore,** Pensacola's pride and joy. On Santa Rosa Island, mile after mile of glistening white sand awaits your arrival. Play in the surf, search for interesting shells, or relax and get a tan. These beautiful beaches and dunes are protected by the government and will be kept in their natural state for future generations of visitors to enjoy.

Panama City Beach is a lively spot during the summer months when temperatures here are cooler than in the rest of the state. If it's action you're looking for, this beach has it!

Did you know?

Geologists have found that the sand here is 99 percent quartz. That's what gives it such a soft and brilliant-white quality.

What's That?

PENSACOLA HISTORIC DISTRICT

Witness Pensacola's colorful history on a walking tour of downtown. The **North Hill Preservation District** is a 60-block area of restored homes dating back to the late 1800s and early 1900s. Don't rush through this area. Take a careful look at the many types of architecture. Each building seems to have a personality of its own. As you wander through the various districts, keep your eyes open for historical markers. They'll tell you of battles and fallen forts that once existed here. You can pick up a walking tour map of this charming area at the Visitor Information Center.

Pensacola's **Seville Preservation District** is equally captivating, with its gardens, tiny shops, and overwhelming peacefulness. The restored homes, specialty shops, and old-time restaurants stretch over 37 blocks. A walking tour will not only give you an idea of what life was like 100 years ago, but will also lead you to some very interesting museums.

Did you know?

Pensacola was settled in 1559, 6 years before St. Augustine. But 2 years later, the Spanish colonists abandoned the settlement after battling hurricanes and Indians. It wasn't until 1752 that Pensacola was established as a permanent settlement.

PENSACOLA NAVAL AIR STATION

High on your list of things to see should be the Pensacola Naval Air Station. It's the largest naval air station in the United States, and it was here that the very first navy fliers were trained for combat in World War I. You won't believe what those old planes looked like unless you've seen one, and you can at the **Naval Aviation Museum.** Witness the growth of flight and space exploration as you walk the time line of historic naval, marine, and Coast Guard aircraft and memorabilia, passing a replica of the navy's first Curtis Biplane, an F6F Hellcat, a Skylab Command Module, and the original prototype of the navy's newest fighter jet, the F-18. But that's not all . . . there's a great display of the evolution of aircraft carriers and a land-survival exhibit that shows you the survival skills course the fliers must pass. Perhaps the most exciting thing of all is when you try your hand at the controls of a jet trainer!

If you're more of a sailor than a flier, you may be in for a special treat. When she's in port, the **USS Lexington**, a huge aircraft carrier, offers free tours of her floating city. During World War II, she was known as the Blue Ghost—the ship that couldn't be sunk.

Also on the grounds of the Pensacola Naval Air Station, along the Gulf Islands National Seashore, is Fort Barrancas, a Confederate fortress that fell to Union forces during the Civil War. It, too, is open to visitors.

Did you know?

The Pensacola Naval Air Station is home to the navy's elite precision-flying team, the Blue Angels. They give a performance twice a year when they aren't on the road.

Did you know?

A U.S. Navy crew circled the Earth for 28 days in the Skylab Command Module in 1973.

The USS *Lexington* is the navy's oldest active carrier. She was commissioned in 1943 and today is primarily used to qualify student and fleet aviators to land aboard a ship.

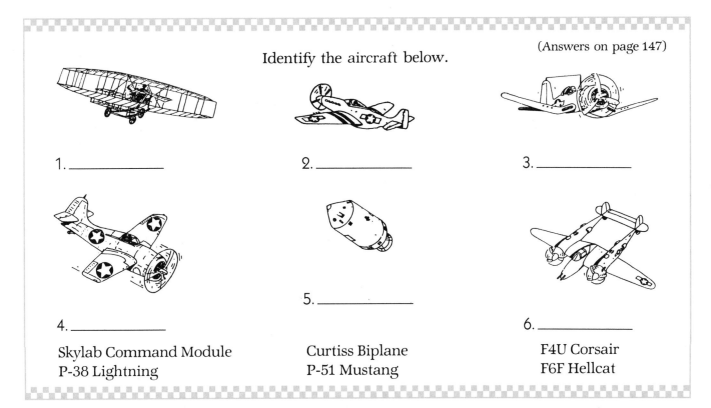

Identify the aircraft below. (Answers on page 147)

1. _____

2. _____

3. _____

4. _____

5. _____

6. _____

Skylab Command Module
P-38 Lightning

Curtiss Biplane
P-51 Mustang

F4U Corsair
F6F Hellcat

FORT PICKENS

Did you know?

Pensacola Naval Air Station isn't the only military installation in the area. Eglin Air Force Base is the largest American air base in the world. It, too, has an aircraft museum to explore.

∎ ∎ ∎

There's a 3rd military base in Northwest Florida. Tyndall Air Force Base, east of Panama City, opened on the day the United States entered World War II.

Prowl the fortress that once imprisoned the fierce Apache chief Geronimo. Fort Pickens can be found on Santa Rosa Island, where it was built in 1829 to protect the naval shipyard on Pensacola Bay. This 5-sided fort took 5 years to build and accommodated as many as 600 men in battle. At the beginning of the War between the States, Fort Pickens went to war against Fort Barrancas on the mainland. Some historians believe that the first shots were fired here, not at Fort Sumter in South Carolina. The Union forces of Fort Pickens triumphed over Fort Barrancas's Confederate force and the city of Pensacola fell into Union hands.

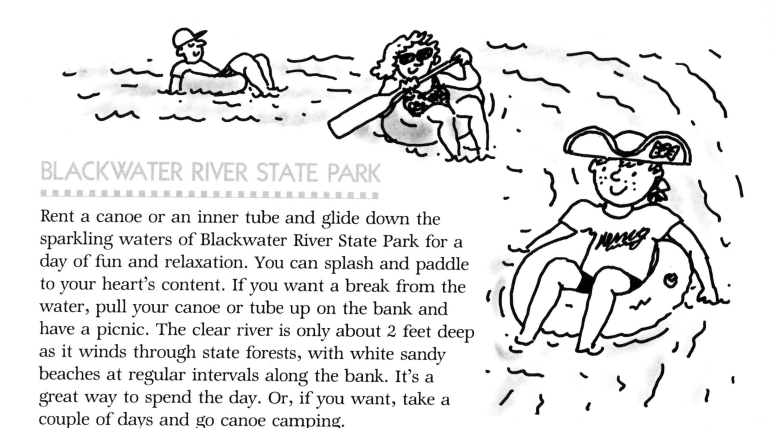

BLACKWATER RIVER STATE PARK

Rent a canoe or an inner tube and glide down the sparkling waters of Blackwater River State Park for a day of fun and relaxation. You can splash and paddle to your heart's content. If you want a break from the water, pull your canoe or tube up on the bank and have a picnic. The clear river is only about 2 feet deep as it winds through state forests, with white sandy beaches at regular intervals along the bank. It's a great way to spend the day. Or, if you want, take a couple of days and go canoe camping.

Did you know?

Blackwater River State Park is the largest of Florida's 4 state forests. You can camp, hike, boat, and fish in this 183,000-acre woodland.

JUNIOR MUSEUM OF BAY COUNTY

You'll be surprised each time you visit the Junior Museum of Bay County in Panama City. It's a diverse museum where exhibits change constantly, so this will seem like a new place every time you visit. Experience a trip back to a turn-of-the-century pioneer farm, where you can see a log cabin, a gristmill, a smokehouse, and a barn full of farm animals. And don't miss a visit to the nature trail, where you'll discover plants and creatures that live in this area. There's also lots of fun classes and hands-on activities to introduce you to the wonders of the natural sciences and art.

T·R·A·V·E·L D·I·A·R·Y

I like museums that have _____, but _____.

I don't like museums that _____.

If I could have my own museum, I'd call it _____,

and inside I would have a collection of _____.

❖ ❖ ❖

FLORIDA CAVERNS STATE PARK

The first thing you'll notice upon entering the Florida Caverns in Marianna is the drop in temperature, so bring a sweater. The cool network of caves 65 feet below the surface is breathtaking. Here formations known as sodastraws, stalactites, stalagmites, draperies, columns, rimstone, and flowstone look like animals, birds, fruit, flowers, and human beings. There's even one formation that looks like a wedding cake!

After a tour of the cavern, take a stroll along one of the nature trails. You may come face-to-face with a beaver, a pileated woodpecker, or an alligator!

Did you know?

The Seminoles may have hidden in these caverns when Andrew Jackson came through in 1818.

TORREYA STATE PARK

East of Marianna is Torreya State Park, a 1,000-acre recreational and botanical park with majestic bluffs overlooking the Apalachicola River. The hiking trails offer extraordinary views of plant life and nature. Local legend has it that this is the site of the biblical Garden of Eden. The Apalachicola River is said to be the world's only "4-headed" river system—just like the one described in the Bible. Also, the torreya tree, which grows on the banks of the river, is said to be the substance Noah used to build his ark.

FLORIDA'S CAPITOL BUILDING

Florida is the fastest-growing state in the nation, and Tallahassee's contemporary 22-story Capitol Building is from where its people are governed. Guided tours leave from the west entrance Welcome Station throughout the day. While you're here, feel free to attend a legislative session (from April to June) or see barristers argue before the judges of the Florida Supreme Court (the first full week of each month, except August and December).

Did you know?

Florida was the first state to open all governmental meetings to the public. This is called the Sunshine Act.

THE MUSEUM OF FLORIDA HISTORY

Visit the past at the Museum of Florida History, a dramatic showcase that brings history to life. Imagine you're a treasure hunter searching for gold doubloons in an old Spanish galleon. Or a steamboat captain navigating your vessel through Florida's waters.

There's a lot here to spark your imagination—arrowheads, Civil War battle flags, "tin can campers," and lots more. Where else can you chat with a giant mastodon?!

Just a short walk from the main museum is the **Old Capitol,** carefully restored to its 1902 appearance. Pretend you're an important politician as you tour the Senate and House Chambers, the Supreme Court, and the Governor's Suite. And don't miss A View from the Capitol, an 8-room exhibit of Florida's political history.

But don't stop there. Wander over to the **Union Bank** across the street. Built in 1841, it's the oldest surviving bank building in Florida. Want to open an account?

You'll have to drive to the last of the museum's sites. It's 3 miles away, but worth the trip. **San Luis Archaeological and Historic Site** stands where an important 17th-century Spanish and Apalachee Indian village once thrived. Stroll the grounds and look at the exhibits telling the story of the people of the village of San Luis de Talimali. If you're here in the spring, you can watch state archaeologists as they unearth the remains of the village.

TALLAHASSEE JUNIOR MUSEUM

Step back in time at the Tallahassee Junior Museum, where 52 acres of nature trails, wildlife exhibits, and the plantation home belonging to Princess Catherine Murat are waiting to be explored. Big Bend Farm, a group of buildings moved here from North Florida

Did you know?

This village was burned by its people as they tried to escape British invaders in 1704.

farms, lets you visualize what life was like on an 1880s homestead, complete with animals. See a blacksmith at work, a sheep being sheared, or syrup being made. The Habitat Trail identifies different kinds of trees, shrubs, and natural features. There's also a Snake Exhibit, Turtle Pond, and lots more. See for yourself.

Did you know?

Most of the animals on the Habitat Trail were orphaned or injured or raised in captivity and probably would not survive if released.

EDWARD BALL WAKULLA SPRINGS STATE PARK

Nature surprises us with her many wonders, and Edward Ball Wakulla Springs State Park is proof of that. One of the world's largest and deepest freshwater springs can be toured aboard a glass-bottom boat in the park. The water is so crystal clear that you'll be able to see the entrance to the cavern 120 feet below, as well as hundreds of native fish that live here.

There's a 45-minute tour of Wakulla Springs' wildlife as well. The boat cruises downstream, passing ancient cypress trees and curious wildlife. If you look very carefully, you may see herons, egrets, turkey vultures, swallow-tailed kites, and even bald eagles. And if you think there's something out there too large to be a bird, look again. It just may be a deer.

Did you know?

The Indians called the spring "mysteries of strange water."

■ ■ ■

Fossilized mastodon bones have been found in the deep of the cavern.

■ ■ ■

Some of the early Tarzan movies were filmed here. So was *Creature from the Black Lagoon*, *Airport 77*, and *Joe Panther*.

Are There Any Animals?

THE ZOO

Meet with over 400 exotic animals in the landscaped gardens of The Zoo, the only land-animal attraction in this area. You'll encounter elephants, tigers, lions, zebras, monkeys, exotic birds, and many other creatures as you hike the trails through the lush botanical gardens. Pet a baby elephant, visit the Wildlife Rescue Center, explore the gift shop. But whatever you do, don't miss feeding time. You've never heard such a racket!

GULFARIUM

Within the gates of Fort Walton's Gulfarium, you'll discover a remarkable world of marine life. Special tanks containing all kinds of sea life offer a rare glimpse at these sometimes unfamiliar creatures. Live porpoises and sea lions give dazzling performances and daring divers swim among manta rays, sharks, and eels at the Living Seas exhibit. It's exciting and terrifying!

127

GULF WORLD

Gulf World in Panama City Beach is a nonstop showcase of marine-animal exhibits and performances. You'll giggle at the hilarious sea lions and gasp as a shark glides by in the walk-through shark tank. And Albert, star of the dolphin show, will delight you with his basketball-playing prowess. If a close-up view of a moray eel is what you're after, be sure to stop at the Coral Reef Theater. It's an underwater zoo where eels and colorful fish swim through their coral home. Scuba divers give informative demonstrations throughout the day, but if you'd like to do more than just look, brave your hand at the Stingray Petting Pool. Once you get your courage up, you'll be glad you did it.

SNAKE-A-TORIUM

Slithery, belly-dragging reptiles may give you the shivers, but at Snake-A-Torium you'll learn to appreciate these often misunderstood creatures. Contrary to what you hear, snakes are not at all slimy. Touch one and find out for yourself. For an interesting show, don't miss the snake-milking performance, where venom is extracted for important medical treatments. But be forewarned: You'll never look at snakes quite the same way again.

Are We Having Fun Yet?

MIRACLE STRIP AMUSEMENT PARK

A coastal amusement park offers loads of fun in Panama City Beach. Hurtle through the twists and turns and ups and downs of the Miracle Strip Amusement Park wooden roller coaster, featuring a thrilling 65-foot drop and dark tunnel. Or get a panoramic view of the beach and ocean from high atop a giant Ferris wheel. And don't miss the tummy-torture of the new Sea Dragon. There's lots of action, from white-knuckler rides and a spooky haunted castle to Junior Hot Rods and the Mini Enterprise for the younger kids. Live entertainment is staged during the summer months, and there are midway games and a huge arcade year-round. It's great fun—day or night!

SHIPWRECK ISLAND

Did anyone ever tell you that you swim like a fish? If so, then Shipwreck Island is the place for you. It's a full day of splashing good fun.

Explore the hole in the bow of the giant shipwreck. Then grab a rope hanging from the yardarm and plunge into the water below. There's a 500,000-gallon wave pool and Tadpole Hole, an area of slides, water cannons, and tunnels for the little kids. Quietly float down the Lazy River Ride and soak up some sun, or summon your courage and shoot the rapids. Whether you like your water fun fast or slow, Shipwreck Island's got what you want.

Did you know?

The Pirate's Plunge water slide can reach speeds of up to 40 mph.

1. What is the capital of Florida?

_____

2. What is the state nickname?

_____

3. What is the state beverage?

_____

4. What is the state flower?

_____

5. What is the largest industry in Florida?

_____

6. In what year did Florida join the United States?

_____

7. Who discovered Florida and when?

_____

8. What is the oldest city in the United States?

_____

9. Who were the 2 millionaires who opened Florida to tourism with their railroads?

_____

10. What is the southernmost city in the continental United States?

_____

11. Where is the best shelling beach in the United States?

_____

12. What city is known for its Cuban cigars?

_____

13. What city is called "the City of Five Flags"?

_____

14. What is the largest tourist attraction in the world?

_____

15. What coast has the whitest beaches?

(Answers on page 148)

Is That All?

Well, isn't Florida a great place to visit? There's something fun to do every minute of the day and no way to see it all on one vacation. You'll have to come back many times to see the places that you've missed, as well as those places that are new or have changed.

Reading up on where you want to go and what you want to see will help you get the most out of every trip. And your travel journal will help you remember what to tell your friends about when you get back home.

For more ideas on what to do in Florida, contact the Florida Department of Tourism or one of the many area chambers of commerce. Nearly every city in Florida has one. And don't forget to ask about special programs for kids at all the parks and museums you visit. Look for colorful guides and brochures at museums, restaurants, and theme parks. A good way to find out about special events for kids is to review the local papers' "Events" sections on Fridays and Sundays. They usually have lists of things for kids to do.

Remember, once you're in Florida, it's a good idea to call ahead to double-check on the places and events you plan to attend. ENJOY!

T·R·A·V·E·L D·I·A·R·Y

I did a lot in Florida. Some places I went to that aren't in

this book are _____. My favorite

thing to do in Florida is _____. If I

come back, I will visit _____, but I won't

visit _____. I liked _____

best because _____.

When I get home, the first thing I will tell my friends is _____

_____. If I have to write about my trip for

school, I will tell my teacher about _____.

The best day of the trip was _____, because

_____that I got at

My favorite souvenir is _____. The next trip I take,

_____.

I want to go to _____.

with _____

❖ ❖ ❖

C·A·L·E·N·D·A·R

JANUARY

Buskerfest, Key West (305) 294-3099
Speed Weeks, Daytona Beach
  (904) 253-6711
Fayre at Vizcaya, Miami (305) 758-8458
International Kite-Flying Contest,
  Sarasota (813) 388-2818
Scottish Highland Games, Orlando
  (407) 647-0782

FEBRUARY

Florida State Fair, Tampa (813) 621-7821
Florida Citrus Festival, Winter Haven
  (813) 293-3175
People's Gasparilla, Tampa
  (813) 223-8518
Gasparilla Invasion and Parade, Tampa
  (813) 228-7338
Edison Pageant of Lights, Fort Myers
  (813) 334-1133
Championship Rodeo, Homestead
  (305) 247-1511
Daytona 500, Daytona Beach
  (904) 253-6711
Silver Spurs Rodeo, Kissimmee
  (407) 847-4052
Old Island Days, Key West
  (305) 294-9501
Ybor City Fiesta Day, Ybor City
  (813) 248-3712

MARCH

Festival of States, St. Petersburg
  (813) 898-3654
Medieval Fair, Sarasota (813) 355-5101
Dade County Youth Fair, Miami
  (305) 223-7060
Sanibel Island Shell Fair, Sanibel Island
  (813) 946-3991
Calle Ocho: Open House 8, Miami
  (305) 324-7349
Major League Baseball Spring Training

APRIL

Easter Week Festival, St. Augustine
  (904) 829-5681
Children's Art Festival, Sarasota
  (813) 355-5101
Sunfest, West Palm Beach (407) 659-5980
Bounty of the Sea Seafood Festival, Miami
  (305) 661-6078
Aqualympics, Miami (213) 784-2630

MAY

International Sandcastle Contest, Sarasota
  (813) 388-2181
Billy Bowlegs Festival, Fort Walton Beach
  (904) 244-8191
Flying High Circus, Tallahassee
  (904) 644-4874
Fiesta of 5 Flags, Pensacola
  (904) 433-3065

JUNE

Sea Turtle Watch, Jensen Beach
  (407) 334-3444
Kissimmee Boat-A-Cade, Kissimmee
  (407) 847-5662
Spanish Night Watch, St. Augustine
  (904) 829-5681
Celebration of Light, Clearwater
  (813) 461-0011
Panhandle Watermelon Festival, Chipley
  (904) 638-1874
Pirate Days, Treasure Island
  (813) 360-0811

JULY

Big Bang, Pensacola (904) 433-3065
God and Country Day, Ocala
   (904) 629-8051
Fourth of July Celebration,
   Jacksonville (904) 249-3868
Blue Angels Air Show, Pensacola
   (904) 433-3065

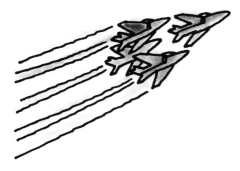

AUGUST

Wausau Fun Day and Possum Festival,
   Wausau (904) 638-1017
Royal Palm Festival, Palm Beach County
   (407) 686-7507

SEPTEMBER

St. Johns River Festival, De Land
   (904) 734-4331
Native American Heritage Festival,
   Tallahassee (904) 576-1636
Anniversary of the Founding of St. Au-
   gustine, St. Augustine (904) 829-5681
Pioneer Florida Day, Dade City
   (904) 567-0262
Oktoberfest, Orlando (407) 422-2434
Great American Raft Race, Port St. Lucie
   (407) 878-4422

OCTOBER

Italian Street Festival, Orlando
   (407) 422-2434
Ocala Week, Ocala (904) 629-2160
Belleview Junction Western Roundup,
   Pensacola (904) 456-5966
Key West Fantasy Fest, Key West
   (305) 294-8585
Country Jubilee, Largo (813) 448-2474

NOVEMBER

Pioneer Days, Orlando (407) 855-7461
Children's Day, Key West (305) 296-2228
National Championship Balloon Race,
   Naples (813) 261-2222
Hollywood Sun 'n Fun Festival,
   Hollywood (305) 920-3330
Blue Angels Air Show, Pensacola
   (904) 433-3065
The Harvest, Miami (305) 375-4694

DECEMBER

Edison Home Holiday House, Fort Myers
   (813) 334-3416
Winterfest and Boat Parade, Fort Lauder-
   dale (305) 522-3983
Christmas Grand Illumination Ceremony,
   St. Augustine (904) 824-8974
Candlelight Processional, Walt Disney
   World (407) 824-4321
St. Johns River Boat Parade, De Land
   (904) 736-7932
Christmas in Lantana, Lantana
   (305) 585-8664
Orange Bowl Festival, Miami
   (305) 642-1515
Junior Orange Bowl Festival, Coral Gables
   (305) 445-7920

A·P·P·E·N·D·I·X

Admission prices and times are continually changing. To be sure of current rates and hours of operation, call ahead.

ADVENTURE ISLAND (813) 971-7978.
4545 Bougainvillea Ave., Tampa 33617. 10:00 A.M.–
10:00 P.M., daily, summer; call for winter hours. $12.95/
person; free/under 2.

ARABIAN NIGHTS (407) 351-5822. W. Irlo Bronson
Hwy. (I-92), Orlando 32819. Call for show times and
admission prices.

ART DECO DISTRICT (305) 672-2014. Miami Design
Preservation League, 12th St. & Washington Ave., Miami
Beach 33139. Ninety-minute tours begin 10:30 A.M., Sat.
$5.00/person.

AUDUBON HOUSE AND GARDENS (305) 294-2116.
205 Whitehead St., Key West 33040. 9:30 A.M.–5:00 P.M.,
daily. $4.50/adult; $1.00/6–12 child; free/under 6.

BALLPARK MEMORIES (904) 824-0515. 3 Aviles St.,
St. Augustine 32084. 10:00 A.M.–6:00 P.M., daily. $2.50/adult;
$1.50/6–12 child; free/under 6.

BELLM'S CARS AND MUSIC OF YESTERDAY
(813) 355-6228. 5500 N. Tamiami Trail, Sarasota 33580.
8:30 A.M.–6:00 P.M., Mon.–Sat.; 9:30 A.M.–6:00 P.M., Sun.
$4.95/adult; $2.25/6–16 child; free/under 6.

BIG CYPRESS NATIONAL PRESERVE
(813) 262-1066. S.R. Box 110, Ochopee 33943. Call or write
for more information.

BILL BAGGS CAPE FLORIDA STATE PARK
(305) 361-5811. Key Biscayne 33149. 8:00 A.M.–sunset, daily.
$1.00/driver; $.50/passenger.

BLACKWATER RIVER STATE PARK (904) 623-2363.
Rte. 1, Box 57-C, Holt 32564. 8:00 A.M.–sunset. $1.00/car.

BOARDWALK AND BASEBALL (407) 648-5151.
I-4 and U.S. 27, Baseball City 33844. 9:00 A.M.–6:00 P.M.,
Sun.–Fri.; 9:00 A.M.–9:00 P.M., Sat. Extended hours summer
& holidays. $17.95/adult; $13.95/child under 48″ & senior
citizen; free/under 3.

BUCCANEER BAY (904) 596-2062. U.S. 19 and S.R. 50,
Weeki Wachee 33512. 10:00 A.M.–5:00 P.M., Mon.–Fri.;
10:00 A.M.–6:30 P.M., Sat. & Sun. Closed Labor Day– Mar.
$5.95/adult; $4.95/3–11 child; free/under 3.

BUSCH GARDENS, THE DARK CONTINENT
(813) 988-5171/(813) 971-8282 (recording). 3000 E. Busch
Blvd., Tampa 33612. 9:30 A.M.–6:00 P.M., daily. Extended
hours summer & holidays. $19.95/person; free/under 2.
Parking $2.00.

**CASTILLO DE SAN MARCOS NATIONAL
MONUMENT** (904) 829-6506. 1 Castillo Dr., St. Augustine
32085. 9:00 A.M.–5:45 P.M., daily, summer; 8:30 A.M.–
5:15 P.M., daily, winter. $1.00/adult; free/senior citizen &
under 13.

CENTRAL FLORIDA ZOOLOGICAL PARK
(407) 323-6471. U.S. 17, 92 at I-4, Sanford 32771. 9:00 A.M.–5:00 P.M., daily. $5.00/adult; $2.00/3–12 child; free/under 3.

CHILDREN'S MUSEUM OF TAMPA (813) 935-8441. 9301 Floriland Mall, Tampa 33612. 10:00 A.M.–5:00 P.M., Tues.–Sat.; 1:00 P.M.–5:00 P.M., Sun. $1.00/2–65; $.75/over 65; free/under 2.

CHURCH STREET STATION (407) 422-2434. 129 West Church St., Orlando 32801. (Includes Rosie O'Grady's Good Time Emporium, Apple Annie's Courtyard, Phineas Phogg's Balloon Works, Lili Marlene's Aviators Pub and Restaurant, Cheyenne Saloon and Opera House.) 11:00 A.M.–2:00 A.M., daily. Free from 11:00 A.M.–5:00 P.M.; $11.95/person from 5:00 P.M.–2:00 A.M.

CONCH TOUR TRAIN (305) 294-5161. Key West 33040. 9:00 A.M.–4:00 P.M., daily. $9.00/adult; $3.00/3–11 child; free/under 3.

CORAL CASTLE (305) 248-6344. 28655 S. Federal Hwy., Homestead 33030. 9:00 A.M.–9:00 P.M., daily. $6.75/adult; $4.50/7–15 child; free/under 7.

CORAL GABLES CHAMBER OF COMMERCE
(305) 446-1657. 50 Aragon Ave., Coral Gables 33134.

CORAL GABLES HOUSE (305) 442-6593. 907 Coral Way, Coral Gables 33134. 1:00 P.M.–4:00 P.M., Sun. & Wed. $1.00/adult; $.50/child.

CORKSCREW SWAMP SANCTUARY (813) 657-3771. C.R. 849/Sanctuary Rd., Naples 33940. Visitors Center open 9:00 A.M.–5:00 P.M., daily. Trail closes at sunset.

CYPRESS GARDENS (813) 324-2111. P.O. Box 1, Cypress Gardens 33880. 9:00 A.M.–7:00 P.M., daily. Special extended hours during peak holiday seasons. $16.95/adult; $11.50/3–11 child; free/under 3.

DOLPHIN RESEARCH CENTER (305) 289-1121. Mile Marker 59, Overseas Hwy., Marathon Shores 33050. Call for

information on Dolphin Encounter (swim) or educational walking tour.

DOLPHIN'S PLUS (305) 451-1993. Mile Marker 100, Overseas Hwy., Key Largo 33037. Call for information.

DREHER PARK ZOO (407) 533-0887. 1301 Summit Blvd., West Palm Beach 33405. 9:00 A.M.–5:00 P.M., daily. Closed Thanksgiving, Christmas, and New Year's Day. $4.00/adult; $2.00/3–12 child & senior citizen; free/under 3.

EAST MARTELLO ART GALLERY AND MUSEUM (305) 296-3913. 3501 S. Roosevelt Blvd., Key West 33040. 9:30 A.M.–5:30 P.M., daily. Last admission 4:15 P.M. $3.00/adult; $1.00/7–15 child; free/under 7.

EDISON WINTER HOME MUSEUM (813) 334-3614. 2350 McGregor Blvd., Fort Myers 33901. 9:00 A.M.–4:00 P.M., Mon.–Sat.; 12:30 P.M.–4:00 P.M., Sun. Closed Thanksgiving and Christmas Day. $5.00/adult; $1.00/6–12 child; free/under 6.

EDWARD BALL WAKULLA SPRINGS STATE PARK (904) 222-7279. S.R. 267 & Florida 61, Wakulla Springs 32305. 8:00 A.M.–sunset, daily. $1.00/driver; $.50/passenger; free/under 6.

EVERGLADES NATIONAL PARK (305) 247-6211. Box 279, Homestead 33030. Park open 24 hours a day. Visitors Center open 8:00 A.M.–4:30 P.M., daily. $5.00/car.

EVERGLADES WONDER GARDENS (813) 992-2591. Old U.S. 41, Bonita Springs 33923. 9:00 A.M.–5:00 P.M., daily. Last tour 4:00 P.M. $5.00/adult; $3.00/5–15 child; free/under 5.

FANTASY ISLES (813) 997-4202. U.S. 41 (N. Tamiami Trail), North Fort Myers 33903. Call for information. Free (rides not included).

FLORIDA'S CAPITOL BUILDING (904) 488-6167. Monroe St. & Apalachee Pkwy., Tallahassee 32301. 9:00 A.M.–4:00 P.M., Mon.–Fri. 11:00 A.M.–3:00 P.M., Sat., Sun., & holidays. Tours leave on the hour. Free.

FLORIDA CAVERNS STATE PARK (904) 482-3632. 2701 Caverns Rd., Marianna 32446. 8:00 A.M.–sunset, daily. $1.00/driver; $.50/passenger. Tour: $2.00/adult; $1.00/6–13 child; free/under 6.

FLORIDA CITRUS TOWER (904) 394-8585. U.S. 27, Clermont 32711. 8:00 A.M.–6:00 P.M., daily. *Tower*: $2.50/adult; $1.75/10–15 student; free/under 10. *Tower & tram*: $4.00/adult; $2.50/10–15 student; free/under 10.

FLORIDA DEPARTMENT OF TOURISM (904) 487-1462. 126 Van Buren St., Tallahassee 32399.

FORT CAROLINE NATIONAL MEMORIAL (904) 641-7155. 12713 Fort Caroline Rd., Jacksonville 32225. 9:00 A.M.–5:00 P.M., daily. Free.

FORT LIBERTY (407) 351-5151. Scott Blvd. & W. Hwy. 192, Kissimmee 32741. Call for show times. $23.95/adult; $15.95/3–11 child.

FORT MYERS HISTORICAL MUSEUM (813) 332-5955. 2300 Peck St., Fort Myers 33901. 9:00 A.M.–4:30 P.M., Mon.–Fri.; 1:00 P.M.–5:00 P.M., Sun. Closed Sat. $2.00/adult; $.50/under 12.

FORT PICKENS (904) 932-5302. Santa Rosa Island. 9:30 A.M.–5:00 P.M., daily, Apr.–Oct.; 8:30 A.M.–4:00 P.M., daily, Nov.–Mar. Closed Christmas Day.

FOUNTAIN OF YOUTH (904) 829-3168. 155 Magnolia Ave., St. Augustine 32085. 9:00 A.M.–4:45 P.M., daily. Closed Christmas Day. $3.50/adult; $2.50/senior citizen & military; $1.50/6–12 child; free/under 6.

GATORLAND ZOO (407) 855-5496/(407) 857-3845. 14501 S. Orange Blossom Trail (U.S. 441), Orlando 32821. 8:00 A.M.–8:00 P.M., summer; 8:00 A.M.–7:00 P.M., winter. $5.40/adult; $3.95/3–12 child; free/under 3.

GULFARIUM (904) 244-5169. U.S. 98, Okaloosa Island, Fort Walton Beach 32548. 9:00 A.M.–6:00 P.M., daily, summer; 9:00 A.M.–4:00 P.M., daily, winter. $8.00/adult; $4.00/4–11 child; free/under 4.

GULF ISLAND NATIONAL SEASHORE (904) 932-5018/(904) 932-5302. P.O. Box 100, Gulf Breeze 32561. $1.00/car.

GULF WORLD (904) 234-5271. 15412 W. Hwy. 98A, Panama City Beach 32407. 9:00 A.M.–7:00 P.M., daily, summer. Call for winter hours. $8.95/adult; $6.95/5–12 child; free/under 5.

HEMINGWAY HOME AND MUSEUM (305) 294-1575. 907 Whitehead St., Key West 33040. 9:00 A.M.–5:00 P.M., daily. $4.00/adult; $1.00/child.

HENRY B. PLANT MUSEUM (813) 254-1891. 401 W. Kennedy Blvd., Tampa 33606. 10:00 A.M.–4:00 P.M., Tues.–Sat. Closed Sun., Mon., & major holidays. Donation requested: $2.00/adult; $.50/child.

HENRY MORRISON FLAGLER MUSEUM (407) 655-2833. Whitehall Way, Palm Beach 33480. 10:00 A.M.–5:00 P.M., Tues.–Sat.; noon–5:00 P.M., Sun. Closed Mon. $3.50/adult; $1.25/6–12 child; free/under 6.

JACKSONVILLE ZOO (904) 757-4462. 8605 Zoo Rd., Jacksonville 32218. 9:00 A.M.–4:45 P.M., daily. $3.00/adult; $1.50/4–12 child; $1.25/senior citizen; free/under 4.

J. N. DING DARLING NATIONAL WILDLIFE REFUGE (813) 472-1100. Sanibel-Captiva Rd., Sanibel 33957. Free.

JOHN PENNEKAMP CORAL REEF PARK (305) 451-1621. Mile Marker 102.5, Overseas Hwy., Key Largo 33037. 8:00 A.M.–sunset, daily. $1.50/driver; $1.00/passenger. Snorkeling, scuba, & boat tours at extra charge. Reservations recommended for all tours.

JUNGLE LARRY'S AFRICAN SAFARI PARK AND CARIBBEAN GARDENS (813) 262-4053. 1590 Goodlette Rd., Naples 33940. 9:30 A.M.–5:30 P.M., daily. Closed Mon. from May–Christmas. $7.95/adult; $5.95/3–15 child; free/under 3.

JUNIOR MUSEUM OF BAY COUNTY (904) 769-6128. 1731 Jenks Ave., Panama City 32405. 9:00 A.M.–4:30 P.M., Mon.–Fri.; 10:00 A.M.–4:00 P.M., Sat. Closed Sun. $1.00 donation requested.

KEY WEST AQUARIUM (305) 296-2051. One Whitehead St., Key West 33040. 10:00 A.M.–6:00 P.M., daily. $5.00/adult; $2.50/8–15 child; free/under 8.

LIGHTHOUSE MILITARY MUSEUM (305) 294-0012. 938 Whitehead St., Key West 33040. 9:30 A.M.–5:00 P.M., daily. Closed Christmas Day. $3.00/adult; $1.00/7–15 child; free/under 7.

LIGHTNER MUSEUM (904) 824-2874. 75 King St., City Hall Complex, St. Augustine 32085. 9:00 A.M.–5:00 P.M., daily. Closed Christmas Day. $3.00/adult; $2.25/military; $1.00/12–18 child; free/under 12.

LION COUNTRY SAFARI (407) 793-1084. Southern Blvd., West Palm Beach 33416. 9:30 A.M.–5:30 P.M., daily. $11.45/adult; $9.95/3–16 child; free/under 3.

LONDON WAX MUSEUM (813) 360-6985. 5505 Gulf Blvd., St. Petersburg 33706. 9:00 A.M.–9:30 P.M., daily. Closed Christmas Day. $4.00/adult; $2.00/5–12 child; free/under 5.

LOWRY PARK ZOO (813) 935-5503. 7525 North Blvd., Tampa 33604. 10:00 A.M.–6:00 P.M., daily. $3.00/adult; $2.00/senior citizen; $1.50/3–12 child; free/under 3.

LOXAHATCHEE NATIONAL WILDLIFE REFUGE (305) 426-2474. S.R. 827, Palm Beach 33480. 6:00 A.M.–8:00 P.M., daily. $3.00/car, Sat. & Sun.; free, Mon.–Fri.

MARINELAND OF FLORIDA (904) 471-1111. S.R. A1A, St. Augustine 32086. 9:00 A.M.–5:30 P.M., daily. $9.95/adult; $4.95/3–11 child; free/under 3.

MEDIEVAL TIMES DINNER AND TOURNAMENT (407) 396-1518. 4510 W. Hwy. 192, P.O. Box 2385, Kissimmee 32742. Call for reservations & show times. The castle is open to the public for free viewing from 9:00 A.M.–4:00 P.M., daily. $25.00/adult; $17.00/3–12 child; free/under 3. (Includes 4-course meal, 2 beverages, & 2-hour performance.)

MEL FISHER'S TREASURE EXHIBIT (305) 296-6533. 200 Greene St., Key West 33040. 9:00 A.M.–5:00 P.M., daily. $5.00/adult; $1.00/under 12.

MGM's BOUNTY (305) 375-0486. Miami Marina, 401 Biscayne Blvd., Miami 33111. Noon–8:00 P.M., Mon.–Thurs.; noon–10:00 P.M., Fri.; 10:00 A.M.–10:00 P.M., Sat.; noon–8:00 P.M., Sun. $3.50/adult; $2.00/senior citizen; $1.50/4–12 child; free/under 4.

MIAMI METROZOO (305) 251-0400. 12400 S.W. 152nd St., Miami 33137. 10:00 A.M.–5:30 P.M., daily. $6.00/adult; $3.00/3–12 child; free/under 3.

MIAMI MUSEUM OF SCIENCE AND SPACE TRANSIT PLANETARIUM (305) 854-4247. 3280 S. Miami Ave., Miami 33129. *Science Gallery:* 10:00 A.M.–6:00 P.M., daily. Closed Christmas & Thanksgiving days. $4.00/adult; $2.50/3–12 child & senior citizen; free/under 3. *Planetarium:* Call the Cosmic Hotline for show times and prices at (305) 854-2222.

MIAMI SEAQUARIUM (305) 361-5703. 4400 Rickenbacker Causeway, Miami 33149. 9:30 A.M.–6:30 P.M., daily. $12.95/adult; $8.95/4–12 child; free/under 4.

MICCOSUKEE INDIAN VILLAGE AND CULTURE CENTER (305) 223-8380. U.S. 41 (Tamiami Trail), Miami 33144. 9:00 A.M.–5:00 P.M., daily. $5.00/adult; $3.50/3–12 child; free/under 3.

MIRACLE STRIP AMUSEMENT PARK (904) 234-3333. 12001 W. Hwy. 98A, Panama City Beach 32407. Hours vary. Please call ahead. $12.00/adult; $10.00/under 11.

MISSION OF NOMBRE DE DIOS (904) 824-2809. San Marco & Old Mission Aves., St. Augustine 32085. 7:00 A.M.–8:00 P.M., daily, summer; 8:00 A.M.–6:00 P.M., daily, winter. *Mass:* 8:30 A.M., Mon.–Fri.; 6:00 P.M., Sat.; 8:00 A.M., Sun.

MONKEY JUNGLE (305) 235-1611. 14805 S.W. 216th St., Miami 33170. 9:30 A.M.–5:00 P.M., daily. $7.50/adult; $4.00/5–12 child; free/under 5.

MUSEUM OF FLORIDA HISTORY (904) 488-1673. R. A. Gray Building, 500 S. Bronough St., Tallahassee 32399. *Museum, Old Capitol, & San Luis Archaeological and Historic Site:* 9:30 A.M.–4:00 P.M., Mon.–Fri.; 10:00 A.M.–4:30 P.M., Sat.; noon–4:30 P.M., Sun. *Union Bank:* 10:00 A.M.–1:00 P.M., Tues.–Fri.; 1:00 P.M.–4:00 P.M., Sat. & Sun. Closed Mon. Free.

MUSEUM OF SCIENCE AND HISTORY (904) 396-7062. 1025 Gulf Life Dr., Jacksonville 32207. 10:00 A.M.–5:00 P.M., Mon.–Thurs.; 10:00 A.M.–10:00 P.M., Fri. & Sat.; noon–5:00 P.M., Sun. $3.00/adult; $2.50/senior citizen; $2.00/4–12 child; free/under 4 & members.

MUSEUM OF SCIENCE AND INDUSTRY (813) 985-5531. 4801 E. Fowler Ave., Tampa 33617. 10:00 A.M.–4:30 P.M., daily. Closed major holidays. $2.00/adult; $1.00/5–15 child; free/under 5.

MUSEUM-THEATER (904) 824-0339. 5 Cordova St., St. Augustine 32084. 9:30 A.M.–5:30 P.M., daily. Closed Christmas Day. *One show:* $2.00/adult; $1.00/6–15 child. *Two shows:* $3.00/adult; $2.00/6–15 child.

NATIONAL KEY DEER WILDLIFE REFUGE (305) 872-2239. Key Deer Blvd. (Florida 940), Big Pine Key 33043.

NATURE CENTER AND PLANETARIUM OF LEE COUNTY (813) 275-3435 (Nature Center)/(813) 275-3183 (Planetarium). 3840 Ortiz Ave., Fort Myers 33905. *Nature Center:* 9:00 A.M.–4:00 P.M., Mon.–Sat.; 11:30 A.M.–4:30 P.M., Sun. $2.00/adult; $.50/under 11. *Planetarium:* Call for show times. $3.00/adult; $2.00/under 11.

OCALA NATIONAL FOREST (904) 625-3147. USDA Forest Service, 227 N. Bronough St., Suite 4061, Tallahassee 32301.

OCEAN WORLD (305) 525-6611. S.E. 17th Street Causeway, Fort Lauderdale 33316. 10:00 A.M.–6:00 P.M., daily. $8.95/adult; $6.95/4–12 child; free/under 4.

OLDEST HOUSE/GONZALES-ALVAREZ HOUSE (904) 824-2872. 14 St. Francis St., St. Augustine 32085. 9:00 A.M.–5:00 P.M., daily. Closed Christmas Day. $3.50/adult; $3.00/senior citizen; $1.75/student; free/under 6.

OLDEST STORE MUSEUM (904) 829-9729. 4 Artillery Ln., St. Augustine 32085. 9:00 A.M.–5:00 P.M., Mon.–Sat.; noon–5:00 P.M., Sun. Closed Christmas Day. $2.50/adult; $2.25/senior citizen; $1.00/6–12 child; free/under 6.

OLD SPANISH QUARTER (904) 824-3355. St. George St., St. Augustine 32085. (Includes 7 restored 18th-century buildings & crafts exhibits. Tickets available at the Gallegos House.) 9:00 A.M.–5:00 P.M., daily. Closed Christmas Day. $2.50/adult; $2.25/senior citizen; $1.50/child & student with ID; free/under 6. Family rate: $5.00.

OLD TOWN TROLLEY (305) 296-6688. Mallory Square, Key West 33040. 8:30 A.M.–4:30 P.M., daily. $9.00/adult; $3.00/6–12 child.

ORLANDO SCIENCE CENTER (407) 896-7151. 810 E. Rollins St., Orlando 32803. 9:00 A.M.–5:00 P.M., Mon.–Thurs.; 9:00 A.M.–9:00 P.M., Fri.; noon–9:00 P.M., Sat.; noon–5:00 P.M., Sun. $4.00/adult; $3.00/4–18 child; free/under 4.

PARROT JUNGLE (305) 666-7834. 11000 W. 57th Ave., Miami 33156. 9:30 A.M.–5:00 P.M., daily. $8.50/adult; $4.00/5–12 child; free/under 5.

PENSACOLA HISTORIC DISTRICT

North Hill Preservation District (Bounded by La Rua, Palafox, Blount & Reus Sts.)

Seville Preservation District (E. Government & S. Alcaniz Sts.)

Visitor Information Center (904) 434-1234. 1401 E. Gregory St., Pensacola 32501. 9:00 A.M.–4:00 P.M., daily.

PENSACOLA NAVAL AIR STATION (904) 452-2311.
3465 Naval Air Station, Pensacola 32508.

Naval Aviation Museum (904) 452-3604. 9:00 A.M.–
5:00 P.M., daily. Closed Thanksgiving, Christmas, & New
Year's days. Free.

USS Lexington (904) 452-3123. 9:00 A.M.–5:00 P.M.,
when in port. Free.

Fort Barrancas (904) 455-5167. 9:00 A.M.–4:00 P.M.,
daily, Nov.–Mar.; 9:30 A.M.–5:00 P.M., daily, Apr.–Oct.
Free.

PLANET OCEAN (305) 361-9455. 3979 Rickenbacker
Causeway, Miami 33149. 10:00 A.M.–6:00 P.M., daily (box
office closes at 4:30 P.M.). $7.50/adult; $4.00/6–12 child;
free/under 6.

POTTER'S WAX MUSEUM (904) 829-9056. 17 King St.,
St. Augustine 32085. 9:00 A.M.–8:00 P.M., daily, summer;
9:00 A.M.–5:00 P.M., daily, winter. $3.95/adult; $3.25/senior
citizen; $2.25/6–12 child; free/under 6.

REPTILE WORLD SERPENTARIUM (407) 892-6905.
5705 E. Bronson Memorial Pkwy., St. Cloud 32769.
9:00 A.M.–5:30 P.M., Tues.–Sun. Closed Sept. $3.75/adult;
$2.75/6–17 child; $1.75/3–5 child; free/under 3.

RINGLING CLOWN COLLEGE (813) 484-0496.
1401 Ringling Dr. S., Venice 33595 (Ringling Brothers and
Barnum & Bailey Circus winter home).

RINGLING MUSEUM COMPLEX (813) 355-5101.
5401 Bayshore Rd., Sarasota 34243. (Includes C'ad'zan, John
and Mabel Ringling Museum of Art, Museum of the Circus,
Asolo Theater.) 10:00 A.M.–6:00 P.M., Fri.–Wed. Closed
Thurs. $5.00/adult; $1.75/6–12 child; free/under 6.

RIPLEY'S BELIEVE IT OR NOT MUSEUM
(904) 824-1606. 19 San Marco Ave., St. Augustine 32085.
9:00 A.M.–8:30 P.M., daily, summer; 9:00 A.M.–6:00 P.M.,
daily, winter. $4.95/adult; $3.95/senior citizen; $2.75/5–12
child; free/under 5.

ST. AUGUSTINE ALLIGATOR FARM (904) 824-3337.
S.R. A1A, St. Augustine 32084. 9:00 A.M.–5:00 P.M., daily.
$5.95/adult; $3.95/3–11 child; free/under 3.

ST. AUGUSTINE SIGHT-SEEING TRAINS
(904) 829-6545. 170 San Marco Ave., St. Augustine 32084.
8:00 A.M.–7:00 P.M., daily, summer; 8:00 A.M.–5:00 P.M.,
daily, winter. Regular tour ticket: $7.00/adult; $2.00/6–12
child; free/under 6. (Does not include attraction admissions;
discount package tours available that include attraction
admissions.)

**ST. AUGUSTINE VISITORS INFORMATION AND
PREVIEW CENTER** (904) 824-3334. 10 Castillo Dr.,
St. Augustine 32085. 8:30 A.M.–5:30 P.M., daily. Film: $2.00/
adult; free/under 16.

SARASOTA JUNGLE GARDENS (813) 355-5305.
3701 Bayshore Rd., Sarasota 33578. 9:00 A.M.–4:30 P.M., daily.
$5.95/adult; $2.95/3–12 child; free/under 3.

SEA WORLD (407) 351-3600. 6277 Sea Harbor Dr.,
Orlando 32821. 8:30 A.M.–9:00 P.M., daily. Special extended
hours during summer & holidays. $23.30/adult; $19.10/3–11
child; free/under 3.

SHELL FACTORY (813) 995-2141. U.S. 41 (N. Tamiami
Trail), North Fort Myers 33903. 9:30 A.M.–6:00 P.M., daily. Free.

SHIPWRECK ISLAND (904) 234-0368. 12001 W. Hwy.
98A, Panama City Beach 32407. 10:30 A.M.–6:00 P.M., daily,
summer. Call for winter hours. $12.00/adult; $10.00/4–10
child; free/under 4 & senior citizen.

SILVER SPRINGS (904) 236-2121. S.R. 40, Silver Springs
32688. 9:00 A.M.–5:30 P.M., daily. $13.95/adult; $8.95/3–11
child; free/under 3.

SIX FLAGS ATLANTIS (305) 926-1000. 2700 Stirling
Rd., Hollywood 33022. Call for park hours. $11.95/adult;
$9.95/3–11 child; free/under 3.

SNAKE-A-TORIUM (904) 234-3311. 9008 W. U.S. 98,
Panama City Beach 32401. 9:30 A.M.–6:00 P.M., daily. $4.70/
adult; $3.70/6–11 child; free/under 6.

SOUTH FLORIDA MUSEUM AND BISHOP PLANETARIUM (813) 746-4132. 201 10th St. W., Bradenton 34205. 10:00 A.M.–5:00 P.M., Tues.–Fri.; 1:00 P.M.–5:00 P.M., Sat. & Sun. Closed Mon. Planetarium shows at 1:30 P.M. & 3:00 P.M., Tues.–Sun. $3.00/adult; $2.00/student. Children under 6 not admitted to planetarium.

SOUTH FLORIDA SCIENCE MUSEUM AND PLANETARIUM (407) 832-1348/(407) 832-1988. 4801 Dreher Trail North, West Palm Beach 33405. 10:00 A.M.–5:00 P.M., Mon.–Sat.; noon–5:00 P.M., Sun. $3.00/adult; $1.50/child.

SPACEPORT USA (407) 452-2121. Visitors Center-TWS, NASA Kennedy Space Center 32899. 9:00 A.M.–7:30 P.M., daily. Closed Christmas Day. (Hours subject to change due to space shuttle launch/landing operations.) *Exhibits, briefings, & grounds:* Free. *IMAX film:* $2.75/adult; $1.75/3–12 child; free/under 3. *Earth Shuttle guided tour:* $4.00/adult; $1.75/3–12 child; free/under 3.

SPONGE EXCHANGE 735 Dodecanese Blvd., Tarpon Springs 33589.

SPONGEORAMA EXHIBIT CENTER (813) 942-3771. 510 Dodecanese Blvd., Tarpon Springs 33589. 10:00 A.M.–6:00 P.M., daily. Free.

SPOOK HILL North Ave. & 5th St., Lake Wales 33853.

SUNCOAST SEABIRD SANCTUARY (813) 391-6211. 18328 Gulf Blvd., Indian Shores 33535. 9:00 A.M.–dark, daily. Free.

SUNKEN GARDENS (813) 896-3186. 1825 4th St. N., St. Petersburg 33704. 9:00 A.M.–5:30 P.M., daily. $5.95/adult; $3.00/3–11 child; free/under 3.

TALLAHASSEE JUNIOR MUSEUM (904) 576-1636. 3945 Museum Dr., Tallahassee 32304. 9:00 A.M.–5:00 P.M., Tues.–Sat.; 12:30 P.M.–5:00 P.M., Sun. Closed Mon. $3.50/adult; $1.50/child.

THEATER OF THE SEA (305) 664-2431. Mile Marker 84.5, Overseas Hwy., Islamorada 33036. Opens 9:30 A.M., daily. Last show starts at 4:30 P.M. $8.50/adult; $5.00/4–12 child; free/under 4. Call for information & prices for dolphin swim.

TORREYA STATE PARK (904) 643-2674. S.R. 271, Rte. 2, Box 70, Bristol 32321. 8:00 A.M.–sunset, daily.

TURTLE KRAALS (305) 294-2640. 200 Margaret St., Key West 33040. Noon–6:00 P.M., daily. Free.

UNIVERSAL STUDIOS FLORIDA (407) 351-7600. 5750 Major Blvd., Orlando 32819. Call for information.

VENETIAN MUNICIPAL POOL (305) 442-6483. 2701 De Soto Blvd., Coral Gables 33134. Call for hours. Closed Mon. $2.85/adult; $1.00/under 12.

VIZCAYA (305) 579-4626/(305) 579-2813. 3251 S. Miami Ave., Miami 33129. 9:30 A.M.–4:30 P.M., daily. Closed Christmas Day. $6.00/adult; $5.00/senior citizen; $4.00/student with ID; free/under 6.

WALT DISNEY WORLD (407) 824-4321. P.O. Box 40, Lake Buena Vista 32830.

Magic Kingdom 9:00 A.M.–10:00 P.M., daily, spring; 9:00 A.M.–midnight, daily, summer; 9:00 A.M.–6:00 P.M., daily, winter. Extended park hours during holidays. *One-day passport:* $28.00/adult; $22.00/3–9 child; free/under 3. Special 3-, 4-, & 5-day world passports available. Parking $3.00.

EPCOT Center 9:00 A.M.–8:00 P.M., daily. Extended park hours during peak seasons and holidays. *One-day passport:* $28.00/adult; $22.00/3–9 child; free/under 3. Special 3-, 4-, & 5-day passports available. Parking $3.00.

River Country 10:00 A.M.–6:00 P.M., daily, spring; 9:00 A.M.–8:00 P.M., daily, summer; 10:00 A.M.–5:00 P.M., daily, winter. Closed Jan. $11.75/adult; $9.25/3–9 child; free/under 3.

Discovery Island   10:00 A.M.–7:00 P.M., daily, summer; 10:00 A.M.–6:00 P.M., daily, winter. $7.50/adult; $4.00/3–9 child; free/under 3.

Typhoon Lagoon, Pleasure Island, Disney/ MGM Studios, Walt Disney World Village
Call for information.

WALTZING WATERS   (813) 267-2533. 18101 U.S. 41 S.E. (San Carlos Park), Fort Myers 33908. 11:00 A.M.–8:00 P.M., daily. $6.70/adult; $3.50/child; free/under 6.

WATER MANIA   (407) 396-2626. 6073 Spacecoast Pkwy. (U.S. 192), Kissimmee 32741. Call for hours of operation. Closed in winter. $10.95/adult; $8.95/3–12 child; free/ under 3.

WEEKI WACHEE   (904) 596-2062. U.S. 19 & S.R. 50, Weeki Wachee 33512. 9:00 A.M.–6:00 P.M., daily. $9.95/adult; $5.95/3–11 child; free/under 3.

WET 'N WILD   (407) 351-3200. 6200 International Dr., Orlando 32819. Call for hours of operation. Closed in winter. $14.95/adult; $12.95/3–12 child; free/under 3.

WILD WATERS   (904) 236-2121. S.R. 40, Silver Springs 32688. 10:00 A.M.–5:00 P.M., Mon.–Fri.; 10:00 A.M.–8:00 P.M., Sat. & Sun. Closed Oct.–Mar. $7.95/adult; $6.95/3–11 child; free/under 3.

WRECKER'S MUSEUM   (305) 294-9502. 322 Duval St., Key West 33040. 10:00 A.M.–4:00 P.M., daily. $2.00/adult; $.50/under 12.

XANADU   (407) 396-1992. 4800 W. Spacecoast Pkwy. (U.S. 192), Kissimmee 32741. 10:00 A.M.–10:00 P.M., daily. $5.95/adult; $3.95/4–17 child; free/under 4.

YBOR CITY STATE MUSEUM/PRESERVATION PARK   (813) 247-6323. 1818 9th Ave., Tampa 33605. 9:00 A.M.–noon and 1:00 P.M.–5:00 P.M., daily. $.50/person.

YBOR SQUARE, LTD.   (813) 247-4497. 1901 N. 13th St., Tampa 33605.

THE ZOO   (904) 932-2229. 5801 Gulf Breeze Pkwy., Gulf Breeze 32561. 9:00 A.M.–6:30 P.M., daily. Closed Thanksgiving & Christmas days. $6.00/adult; $3.50/3–11 child; free/ under 3.

ZOOVET PRODUCTIONS   (305) 743-7000. Hawk's Cay Resort, Mile Marker 61, Overseas Hwy., Marathon 33050. Call for information.

ZORAYDA CASTLE   (904) 824-3097. 83 King St., St. Augustine 32085. 9:00 A.M.–9:00 P.M., daily, summer; 9:00 A.M.–5:30 P.M., daily, winter. $3.00/adult; $2.25/senior citizen & military; $1.50/6–15 child; free/under 6. Local residents: $.50/adult; $.25/child.

C·A·R G·A·M·E·S

Long car rides don't have to be boring or drive you crazy. Playing games will make the time fly. You don't have to sit still and get sore, stiff, and restless either. Stretch out and move your tired muscles with some easy car exercises. They'll keep you from wishing you could roll down the window and scream or kick open the door and jump out.

Games are for fun, so laugh it up and play the ride away.

Things to take along on any long ride: something hard and flat to write on—like a tray, board, or large hardcover book

> coloring pens, pencils, or crayons
> pad of paper or notebook
> deck of cards
> books to read

WORD GAMES:

Think of as many names as you can for each letter of the alphabet.
D: Debbie, Doug, Diane, Denise, Dan, and so on.

Look for each letter of the alphabet on car license plates as they pass (you can skip the hard-to-find letters Q and Z).

Make words out of the letters you see on car license plates.
For example, for 125 BHV, say "beehive."

Packing for your trip: Name things you can put in your suitcase starting with the letter A, then B, then C, and so on.
For example: Apple, Baseball, Cat, Dictionary (they don't really *have* to be things you need on your trip).

COUNTING GAMES:

Watch car license plates and count the numbers, starting with zero. See who can reach 9 first. Or keep counting to 20—it takes longer.

Find the most: Pick something to count and see who can find the most. You can pick things like green cars, stop signs, license plates from California, people driving with hats on, kids in cars, and so on.

GUESSING GAMES:

20 Questions: Think of something for the others to guess. They ask you questions to try to figure out what it is. You can only answer "yes" or "no." If no one guesses in 20 questions, you win. Or you can just let them keep asking questions until someone figures it out.

Pictionary (like dictionary, but with pictures): Like 20 Questions, someone is "It" and thinks of something that everyone else tries to guess. You draw pictures to give them clues and hints—but you can't draw what the answer is. You could pick the name of your school. Then, for clues, you could draw your classroom, desk, schoolbook, lunch box, or teacher—or anything else you might think of. Draw pictures until someone guesses what it is you're thinking of.

DRAWING:

One person draws a mark, line, shape, letter, or number, and someone else has to make a picture out of it.

STORIES:

One person starts to make up a story. The next person has to add the next line or sentence to the story; then on to the next person. Everyone in the car takes a turn making up the story line-by-line. It can turn out to be a pretty funny story. You might even end up on the moon with a _____ .

Make up a travel friend: This is your chance to say anything you want about your trip. You pretend that you have an invisible friend taking the trip with you. Only you can see and hear your friend, so you have to tell everyone else what your friend is saying. Does he or she like your car? Where does she want to go tomorrow? What does he like to eat? You can say ANYTHING. Make up a story about where your friend is from, what his or her family is like—or whatever you want.

CARDS:

Bring along a deck of cards and play your favorite games. Or, if there's room, you can turn a hat over and try to toss the cards into it. You have to throw them as if they were tiny Frisbees.

MOVEMENT GAMES:

Charades: Someone acts out a kind of animal (or anything else) using only face and hands.

Everyone else has to guess what she or he is.

Simon Says: Choose someone to be Simon. Everyone else has to do whatever Simon says—but only when Simon says, "Simon says . . . ." If Simon doesn't say this and you do what he or she says, you goof. Like this: "Simon says, 'Touch your nose with your right hand.' " (Simon touches his nose. Everyone else does, too.) Simon gives lots of directions, then he sneaks in an order without saying "Simon says" but does it anyway. If anyone follows, he or she goofs.

Statue: Everyone playing this game freezes into a statue. See who can stay that way the longest without moving.

Making Faces: Someone is "It." He or she makes a face—sad, goofy, happy, sleepy, cranky—and the other person has to imitate the face. This simple game is really a crack-up.

EXERCISES:

You'll be amazed at how much exercise you can get while riding in a car. You can't swim, run, or throw a ball, but you can work out by stretching your muscles. Make up your own stretches, or do the ones below. Remember to hold one stretch to the count of 10 before beginning another. And don't forget to take a deep breath and blow it out slowly with every stretch. It's "car yoga."

Touch your toes. Stretch your arms straight out. Spin them in circles. Twist around as far as you can. Reach for the ceiling. Bend your head backward. Bend it forward. Press your hands down on the seat next to you and try to lift yourself off the seat. Flex your feet up, then down; point your toes. Repeat this 10 times. You'll be surprised at how good this feels for stiff muscles.

Answers to Puzzles

page 19

			¹P							
²S		³O	S	C	E	O	L	A		
E		N								
M		⁴C	I	V	I	L	W	A	⁵R	
I		E							A	
N		D			⁶S	P	A	I	N	
⁷F	O	R	T	M	Y	E	R	S		
L		L			⁸C	I	T	R	U	S
⁹H	E	N	R	Y				O		
		¹⁰T	O	U	R	I	S	M		
		N						A		
								D		

page 36

Zorayda Castle
Ballpark Memories
Fountain of Youth
Castillo de San Marcos

Lightner Museum
Potter's Wax Museum
Old Spanish Quarter
Oldest Store Museum

page 35

page 38

Mercury
Venus
Earth
Mars
Jupiter

Saturn
Uranus
Neptune
Pluto

page 50

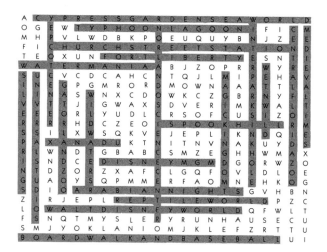

page 53

Bashful, Doc, Dopey, Grumpy, Happy, Sleepy, Sneezy

page 54

1. Fantasyland
2. Main Street, U.S.A.;
   Tomorrowland; Fantasyland;
   Adventureland; Liberty
   Square; Frontierland
3. Here are some: *Dumbo, Lady
   and the Tramp, Fantasia,
   Snow White and the Seven
   Dwarfs, Bambi, Cinderella,
   101 Dalmations, The Aristocats*
4. World Showcase and
   Future World
5. Experimental prototype
   community of tomorrow

page 57

page 70

15	panther	20	zebra
5	elephant	12	monkey
7	hippopotamus	16	rhinoceros
19	wallaby	17	tiger
11	llama	4	black bear
6	giraffe	3	armadillo
18	tortoise	9	Key deer
10	lion	14	panda
2	anteater	1	alligator
8	jaguar	13	orangutan

page 77

page 81

penny stuck in cement → Mallory Pier
wildlife paintings → Hemingway Home and Museum
submarine periscope → Lighthouse Military Museum
early cigar labels → East Martello Art Gallery and Museum
gold doubloon → Mel Fisher's Treasure Exhibit
mimes & jugglers → Audubon House

page 88

1. pelican
2. egret
3. macaw
4. flamingo
5. anhinga
6. great white heron

page 104

1. Little Miss Muffet
2. Little Jack Horner
3. Little Boy Blue
4. Little Bo-Peep
5. Queen of Hearts
6. The Three Little Kittens
7. Wee Willie Winkie
8. Georgie Porgie
9. Peter, Peter Pumpkin-Eater
10. Mary, Mary, Quite Contrary

page 95

1. conch
2. tulip
3. scallop
4. junonia
5. common clam
6. olive

Univalves: junonia, tulip, olive, conch
Bivalves: common clam, scallop

page 121

1. Curtiss Biplane
2. P-51 Mustang
3. F4U Corsair
4. F6F Hellcat
5. Skylab Command Module
6. P-38 Lightning

1. Tallahassee
2. The Sunshine State
3. Florida orange juice
4. Orange Blossom
5. Tourism
6. 1845
7. Ponce de León in 1513
8. St. Augustine
9. Henry B. Plant and Henry Morrison Flagler
10. Key West
11. Sanibel Island
12. Ybor City
13. Pensacola
14. Walt Disney World
15. The West Coast

PHOTO CREDITS

I·N·D·E·X

150